THE NEW INTERNATIONAL COMMENTARY ON THE
NEW TESTAMENT   —F. F. BRUCE, *General Editor*

THE EPISTLE OF PAUL TO THE
CHURCHES OF GALATIA

THE EPISTLE OF PAUL TO THE CHURCHES OF GALATIA

THE ENGLISH TEXT WITH INTRODUCTION, EXPOSITION AND NOTES

by

HERMAN N. RIDDERBOS

Professor of New Testament
Kampen Theological Seminary
Kampen, The Netherlands

WM. B. EERDMANS PUBLISHING CO.
GRAND RAPIDS, MICHIGAN

Set up and printed, April, 1953
Fourth printing, September, 1965

BS
2685
R5

The manuscript of this volume
was translated from the Dutch by
Henry Zylstra, Ph.D.

PHOTOLITHOPRINTED BY CUSHING - MALLOY, INC.
ANN ARBOR, MICHIGAN, UNITED STATES OF AMERICA

General Foreword

Wherever the Dutch language is read Professor Herman Ridderbos is recognized as an outstanding New Testament scholar and theologian, and thus it is gratifying to be able to introduce him to English readers through the medium of this new commentary. After serving as pastor of churches for eight years, in 1943 he became professor of New Testament studies in the Kampen Theological School of the Reformed Churches of the Netherlands. He thus succeeded Dr. S. Greijdanus who had been one of his instructors during his undergraduate days at Kampen.

Specializing at the Free University of Amsterdam under Professor F. W. Grosheide, whose commentary on I Corinthians in this series has just been published, Ridderbos qualified for his doctor's title in 1936 with a distinguished dissertation on the Sermon on the Mount (*De Strekking der Bergrede naar Matthëus*). Among his notable publications mention may be made especially of his excellent commentary on Matthew in two volumes (in the *Korte Verklaring* series, 2nd edit., 1952) and his monumental work on the Kingdom of God (*De Komst van het Koninkrijk*, 1950). A recent brief introduction to the study of Paul (*Paulus en Jezus*, 1952) marks a transition of interest from his earlier concentration upon the Gospels, and the present work on Galatians will be welcomed as another evidence of his fruitful concern with the apostle Paul.

Dr. Herman Ridderbos also plays an active part in the ecclesiastical and religious life of the Netherlands. He is constantly active as preacher, lecturer and contributor to various magazines including especially *Het Gereformeerd*

5

Weekblad, a weekly organ of comment and opinion which is widely read in the Netherlands.

The Ridderbos name has long been synonymous with eminent Biblical scholarship. Dr. Jan Ridderbos, father of our author, was professor of Old Testament studies at Kampen for nearly forty years until his recent retirement, and a brother, Dr. N. H. Ridderbos, has recently been installed as professor in the same field at the Free University of Amsterdam as the successor of Dr. G. Ch. Aalders.

There is perhaps no part of the New Testament, and certainly no epistle of Paul, which offers a greater challenge to the modern expositor than the Epistle to the Galatians. And by the same token no work of interpretation, if it is really well done, can make a greater contribution to the understanding of the message of the New Testament than one devoted to this extraordinary epistle. It is doubtful whether any letter has stirred up more controversy and at the same time has affected more decisively the estimate that men have formed of the Christianity of the New Testament. How this explosive and fiery communication must have overwhelmed its first readers and have removed any doubt as to Paul's understanding of the gospel and its practical implications for the issues that had arisen among them! And because it is concerned with some of the most profound questions of human existence and destiny, it has been recognized as possessing extraordinary contemporaneity and dynamic force in our own modern times in spite of the distinctiveness of the situation addressed and the particularity of many details of its contents. The place which it occupied in shaping Luther's fresh insight into the gospel and in influencing his exposition of the Christian message provides notable evidence of its relevancy in times far removed from the first Christian century. During the past century no writing of Paul has been more of a battle ground in the debate concerning the meaning of

Paul and the precise place he occupied in early Christianity. And though Paul has not proved to be as congenial to our modern age as to Luther and the Reformers generally, there remains the hope that his message of the grace of God, allowing of no adulteration with a religion of works, will again cause the lamp of liberty in Christ to blaze up with new power and life. It is the prayer of the editor that this fresh and stimulating new exposition of Galatians may make a significant contribution to that end.

N. B. STONEHOUSE
General Editor

Philadelphia, Pa.
March 15, 1953

Note: Upon the death of Ned B. Stonehouse, November 18, 1962, F. F. Bruce accepted the publishers' invitation to become General Editor of this series of New Testament commentaries begun under the very able and faithful scholarship of Professor Stonehouse.

The Publishers

ABBREVIATIONS

ASV — American Standard Version (1901)

Bl.-Debr. — Grammatik des neutestamentlichen Griechisch (Blass-Debrunner)

HRE — Real-encyclopädie für protestantische Theologie und Kirche (Hauck-Herzog)

ICC — International Critical Commentary

LXX — The Septuagint

SPA — Sitzungsberichte der Preussischen Akademie der Wissenschaften

TWNT — Theologisches Wörterbuch zum Neuen Testament (Kittel)

CONTENTS

PART TWO: THE GOSPEL OF JUSTIFICATION
BY FAITH ALONE MAINTAINED OVER AGAINST THE
JUDAIZER'S CHALLENGE — 3:1-5:12

PART THREE: THE NEW LIFE THROUGH
THE HOLY SPIRIT — 5:13-6:10

INTRODUCTION

THE EPISTLE OF PAUL TO THE CHURCHES OF GALATIA

INTRODUCTION

I

The Relationships between Paul and the Galatians According to the Data of the Epistle

The churches of Galatia, to whom Paul is addressing himself in this epistle (1:2), were churches which he himself had founded (1:8, 9; 4:19). The apostle speaks of the considerable effort which his labor with them had cost him (4:11). The first time he preached the gospel to them he did so while suffering from, or in consequence of, a physical infirmity or ailment (4:13). This infirmity, Paul writes, constituted a temptation for them to turn away from him in disgust; but, so far from shunning him for that reason, they had received him as an angel of God, indeed, as Christ Jesus Himself. The letter tells us nothing more specific about the nature of this disease (see the Exposition). What we are to think about it depends partly upon which churches we suppose are being addressed in the letter. If we think these are the churches in the Roman provinces of Galatia, we can find in Acts 13:50, 51; 14:6, 7, and 2 Timothy 3:11 a significant hint as to the nature of this physical condition (see Introduction, IV).

We can deduce from Galatians 1:8 that Paul was in the company of others when he preached the gospel to them. Who these others were, and, indeed, whether his company consisted of one or more persons, cannot be made out from the letter itself. That is again a problem whose solution depends upon which churches we think are being addressed. If we conclude that they are the churches of

North Galatia, then Silas and Timothy are candidates for consideration; if, however, the churches of South Galatia are being addressed, then Barnabas may have been the person with Paul.

It would seem to follow from 4:13 that the apostle had more than once visited the churches addressed in the letter. True, some commentators construe the passage translated as *the first time* in our version in a different way. They make it read *before* or *formerly*. This is a construction which of course rules out the implication that Paul had visited the churches of Galatia more than once. The context, however, pleads for the translation: *the first time* (see the Exposition). We conclude, therefore, that the apostle visited the churches of Galatia at least once after their founding. This matter plays a considerable role in ascertaining the date of the letter (Introduction, V).

It is important, further, to establish the fact that these churches were converted by the preaching of Paul from heathendom. This follows clearly from such a passage as 2:5, in which the apostle speaks of his endeavor for the Gentiles, and of how, in this effort, he wanted also to serve the interests of the Galatians ("with you"). It follows also from 4:8, where the former religion of the churches is expressly referred to. And it follows, finally, from Paul's reiterated warning that they ought not to let themselves be circumcised (5:2; 6:12). This does not, of course, rule out the likelihood that there were Jews in the churches of Galatia, just as was the circumstance in practically all of the churches founded by Paul. At least it is clear that the apostle assumes a more than superficial knowledge and grasp of the Jewish religion on the part of his readers: witness, for instance, his disquisitions on the law in Chapter 3, and his allegory of Sarah and Hagar in Chapter 4. Such an orientation is most plausibly explained on the assumption that there were Jews in the places where the churches were founded, and also in the churches themselves.

II

Occasion and Purpose

The occasion for the writing of this letter was something which had come up in the churches of Galatia since Paul's last visit there. Within a short time (cf. 1:6) they had allowed themselves to be brought around to another doctrine than that which Paul had once and again preached to them. True, he had previously warned them against the danger to which they had now fallen victim (cf. 1:9). At that time, however, he had not yet noticed any signs of the change which was now materializing. Hence the surprise to which he gives expression in 1:6.

The heretical teachers who were responsible for this change (cf. 1:7; 5:10, 12; 6:12, 13) taught that circumcision was necessary for salvation (5:2; 6:12 ff.), and they accordingly demanded a maintenance of the ceremonial law of Moses, or at least the observation of days and months and seasons and years (4:10; cf. 4:21). Unquestionably these teachers claimed for themselves the name of Christian and held that they faithfully preached the gospel (cf. 1:6). However, they not only modified this teaching with heresies so serious that Paul denies to their doctrine the name of gospel (1:7), but they also in their teaching acted out of false motives: that is, out of personal ambition (cf. 4:17; 6:13) and out of offense at the cross of Christ (6:12).

Further, these erring teachers did not scruple to cast suspicion upon Paul's qualifications for the office and ministration of an apostle. Paul, at least, finds it necessary to declare that in his preaching he seeks to please, not men, but God (1:10); that he was called to his office, not by men, but by God Himself (1:1, 12) and in a most unexpected way at that (1:13); further, that he was not dependent for his knowledge of the gospel upon the other apostles, but that, on the contrary, he had gotten his commission and insight directly from the Lord (1:12, 16 ff.); and that, later, when he came into contact with the other apostles, he maintained his independence over against them, as might be seen from the circumstance of Titus' remaining uncircumcised and from Paul's altercation with Peter at Antioch (cf. 2:1 ff., 6-10). At the same time Paul makes it very clear that there was full agreement between him and the other apostles on the score of the principles of missions to the heathen (cf. 2:7-10), so that the errant teachers can lodge nothing against him, either on the count of his independence or on that of certain deviations from the other apostles.

Finally, the apostle rejects the charge that he might, if time and occasion suggested it, himself again preach the circumcision (5:11). In short, everything seems to point to the fact that the heretical teachers were trying to discredit Paul personally, and so to make him suspect in the churches he had established.

It is now generally agreed that the misguided teachers here being counteracted were Judaizers, that is, Jewish Christians who wanted to combine the gospel of Christ with the observation of Jewish ceremonies — a position which had been rejected at the so-called apostolic council at Jerusalem. Some, it is true, have wanted to deduce from 5:10 that the heretical influence came up under the leadership of one person, someone, namely, who carried considerable weight. Moreover, it might be inferred from the distinction made between the earthly and the heavenly Jerusalem (4:21-31), the first being the mother of the fleshly seed of Abraham, and the other of the spiritual seed, that Jewish-Christian missionaries had come to

Galatia from Jerusalem. All this is uncertain, but it is not impossible.

That is more than can be said for the idea represented by Edward Meyer in his *Ursprung und Anfänge des Christentums*, III, 1923, page 434, which has it that the person indicated in 5:10 is Peter, and that this fact accounts for the passion with which Paul defends himself in this letter. This idea goes back to the contentions of the old Tübingen school. It is an idea which conflicts, however, not only with what we are told in the Acts of the Apostles concerning Peter's position on the matter in question (*cf.* Acts 10:34; 11:4 ff.; 15:6 ff.), but which conflicts also with the testimony of the letter to the Galatians itself. For, though it is true that Paul in Galatians 2:11 ff. speaks of his difference from Peter about the observance of the ceremonial law, everything points to the fact that Peter and Paul essentially agreed in principle on the matter, and that Peter, at a weak moment, hesitated to assume the consequences of that principle.

The heresy which Paul is counteracting in this letter is, however, of quite a different nature, and it is this fact which gives the letter its passionate tone. Personal rivalry between Paul and Peter is not at all in question here. Quite as unacceptable is the hypothesis developed by H. Lietzmann in his *Die Reisen des Paulus* (SBA), 1930, page 153 ff., and in his commentary *An die Galater* (3), 1932, page 38. Lietzmann there maintains that Paul's real opponent in this letter is none other than Barnabas. For this position, too, there is no basis in the text of the letter. As a matter of fact, the way in which Barnabas is brought into the discussion in 2:1, 9 argues directly against such a construction. Instead therefore of adopting these and other interpretations which do violence to the record, we hold to the data lying ready at hand in the letter. These

17

tell us plainly of the Judaistic heresy, without designating specifically who its propagators were.

Another interpretation of the heretical teachers being combatted in Galatians, and thence of the whole bearing of the letter, has it that Paul is not taking to the field against the Judaistic threat merely, but against heathen libertinism also. This view is sometimes called the two-front theory. It is a view which has been advocated by W. Lütgert, in his *Gesetz und Geist,* 1919, and by J. H. Ropes in "The Singular Problem of the Epistle to the Galatians," *Harvard Theological Studies,* XIV, 1929. This construction has not met with much acceptance: it involves too hypothetical a conception of conditions in the Galatian churches; it is not necessary in order to explain the paraenetic portion of the letter; and it is hard to harmonize with the first portion of it.

Accordingly, we hold to the traditional view that Paul is here combatting a Judaistic Christianity which had infiltrated the churches of Galatia from without, in an attempt to cut off the effect of Paul's work and to supplant it by the Judaizing interpretation of Christianity. Within a short while this heresy had deeply influenced the churches. They were shaken in their conviction (1:7; 5:10, 11), they seemed bewitched (3:1), and they had begun to depart from the gospel which had been preached to them (1:6).

Such being the state of affairs, and the report of it having come to Paul's attention, he had no choice but to intervene. He does so in a singularly passionate way, so that the letter to the Galatians, more than any other of the apostle's extant writings, gives us some idea of his fiery temperament. However, it gives us an insight also into the serious threat which this heresy spelled for the purity of the gospel and the welfare of the church.

III

Content and Character

After a very brief and soberly restrained *exordium* and salutation, in which Paul immediately, and with impressive force, maintains the unassailability of his apostolic calling (1:1-5), he at once expresses his surprise that the Galatians should so hastily have embraced another gospel. He denies to this new teaching the name of gospel, and he pronounces an anathema against any and all, whoever they be, that preach another gospel than the one he brought them (1:6-9).

For the rest, the letter can be divided into three parts, in which the apostle, approaching the matter from three different directions, defends the truth of his gospel against the attacks that have been made upon it.

(1) 1:10-2:21. This part is concerned mainly with Paul's apostolic qualifications — qualifications which had obviously been challenged by the Judaizers. In reply, the apostle points to his direct calling by God; to his independence from the other apostles; to his defense of the gospel of grace at Jerusalem, and to the recognition accorded him by the leaders of the church there; and, finally, to his fearless correction of Peter when the latter faltered and so threatened the purity of the gospel. From all this the legitimacy of Paul's qualifications as an apostle must become evident, and also the unassailability of the authority to which he lays claim.

(2) 3:1-5:12. This constitutes the letter proper, so to speak. In it the material difference between the gospel and the Judaistic heresy is brought to light, and the latter is strongly attacked. Apparently again in refutation of the contentions of the false teachers, Paul here indicates that, if one is to be called a child of Abraham and to share in his promises, he must seek salvation not in the works

of the law but in faith. As counterpart to this, Paul points to the true significance of the law, and to the freedom of believers from the law, something which the apostle presses hard upon the Galatians in view of their incomprehensible falling away from the true gospel.

(3) 5:13-6:8. In this last part, Paul shows that this freedom from the law may not become an occasion for license. Thereupon the life of freedom in the Spirit is discussed in detail, and is set in contrast to the works of the flesh. The letter ends with a final warning against the false teaching, and with a personal appeal to the Galatians by the apostle that they remain true to the gospel of Christ.

* * *

From the resumé given above of the main contents of the letter its character also becomes evident. In character the letter to the Galatians most resembles that to the Romans. All the same, commentators have not without reason pointed out a difference in shading between Paul's treatment of the law in the letter to the Romans and his treatment of it in the letter to the Galatians.

In the Galatian letter the whole emphasis falls on the negative significance of the law. Witness 3:10: all who look for hope to the works of the law are under the curse; 3:12: living out of the law is not ancillary to living out of faith, but antithetical to it; 3:19: the function of the law consists in this, that it brings transgression to light and, so to speak, arouses the sense of it; moreover, the law was not given to Israel by God Himself in His own person, as the promise was given to Abraham by the Lord Himself, but it was ordained through angels by the hand of a mediator — a significant token of the comparative worth of the two; 3:21: the law cannot "make alive"; 3:23 ff.: it must therefore be carefully distinguished as preliminary and provisional in character, its service being to hold men securely in ward against the coming of Christ, and, like a severe and exacting schoolmaster, to drive them to Christ; 3:25 ff.: since Christ has come, however, the law has lost this function and believers are in that sense now free from its tutelage. To those who would look to the law for the possibility of salvation, the law can only mean captivity, slavery, and the want of freedom. From such bondage Christ has purchased the liberation of His own in order to establish them in the rank of sons of God — a truth which becomes evident also from the allegory of Hagar and Sarah in 4:21-31.[1]

In the letter to the Romans also this negative significance of the law comes in for some attention, as when we read that the law works wrath (Rom. 4:15), and that it serves to make trespass abound (Rom. 5:20); but in this letter in general it is the loftiness and holiness of the law of God that is placed in the foreground — a loftiness and holiness which failed of their purpose only by reason of the sin of men (*cf.* Rom. 7 *passim*). Some have construed this difference between Galatians and Romans as expressive of a change of mind, and these maintain that in the interim between the two letters Paul must have arrived at an entirely different idea of the law. There is no occasion, however, for such a judgment. In the first place, Galatians makes it very plain, too, that the law is of divine origin (3:19), that it also is an evidence of God's grace (3:21), and that, despite all its severity, it was intended, nevertheless, to make room for Christ (3:23 ff.). Such considerations serve to enhance the high importance and the holy character of the law. In the second place, it must be remembered that in the letter to the Galatians, as distinguished from the one to the Romans, the whole argu-

---

[1] See also for this entire problem of freedom and the law, my "Vrijheid en Wet volgens Paulus' Brief aan de Galaten," an essay contributed to *Arcana Revelata*, the volume published in honor of F. W. Grosheide (1951) pp. 89-104.

ment is governed by Paul's difference from the Judaizers, who wanted to bind the believers to the ceremonies of Moses also after the advent of Christ. It is altogether natural, therefore, that in such an orientation of meaning, the provisional and negative significance of the law should occupy the foreground. In the letter to the Romans, meanwhile, the argument is more balanced, is slanted less towards the dangers of keeping the law, and is oriented more towards its positive and permanent significance.

We can therefore say that what is indicated in the letter to the Galatians is *the inadequacy of the law for salvation,* and that what gets the emphasis in the letter to the Romans is this: that there is salvation *despite the transgression of God's holy law.*

IV

The Churches That Are Being Addressed

With regard to the problem of who is being addressed in this letter, that is, where the *churches of Galatia* mentioned in 1:2 are to be found, two theories have been advanced. These are the so-called North Galatian and South Galatian theories.

According to the first or North Galatian theory, the term Galatia must be taken to refer to the *geographical territory* of that name which lay in the heart of Asia Minor, and was bounded on the north by Pontus and Bithynia, on the southwest by Phrygia, and on the east by Cappadocia. It had gotten its name from the Celtic tribes of Tectosages, Tolistobogii, and Trocmi, which had infiltrated from Macedonia and Thessaly in the third century before Christ, and it comprised as its principal cities those of Ancyra, Pessinus, and Tavium. The inhabitants of this territory were, in distinction from the West-European Celts, called the Gallograecians. They constituted a very heterogeneous element of the Asiatic peoples and for a long time pre-

served their own customs and peculiarities. Even after
centuries had passed, a deep gulf separated them from sur-
rounding peoples.

Since ancient times it has been accepted that it was to the
believers among these Galatian people that he wrote his
letter. About the middle of the eighteenth century, however, the so-called South Galatian hypothesis was developed, according to which Galatia must be taken to refer
to the Roman *province* of that name, which comprised in
addition to the territory named above also the territories
of Pisidia, Lycaonia, and parts of the regions of Phrygia
and Cappadocia. In other words, according to this theory,
the Galatia of the letter included also the cities of Antioch,
Lystra, Derbe, and Iconium — places which Paul visited
on his first and second missionary journeys. We have a
far more vivid impression of the churches at these places,
an impression gathered, of course, from the Acts of the
Apostles, than we have of those in the North Galatian area.

The strongest arguments for the so-called South Galatian hypothesis are the following:

(1) Paul, in distinction from Luke in the Acts of the
Apostles, always, or almost always, uses the names of the
Roman provinces rather than those of the original geographical territories for the places he has visited.[2] It is
true that this argument is sometimes attacked by reference
to such passages as Galatians 1:22 and others, where
Judaea is mentioned, although it is not certain whether this
Judaea in the Roman sense represents the whole of Palestine or some more restricted area. In the first place,
this stricture therefore at best points to an uncertainty;
and, in the second place, even if Judaea here refers to a
more restricted territory, such an exception would not
prove much against the general rule. It would be quite
possible that such a native Jew as Paul would in such an

---

[2] Cf. Th. Zahn, *Einleitung in das N. T.*, I, 3rd edit. (1924) pp.
124 and 131ff.

instance retain the long-established and traditionally employed name of the territory, whereas for the rest he consistently used the Roman provincial names. Similarly, the other so-called "exceptions," *e.g.,* the reference to Arabia in Gal. 4:25, to Achaia in 2 Cor. 1:1 and 1 Cor. 16:15, and to Cilicia in Gal. 1:21, are highly doubtful. The facts are that, wherever we can judge with absolute certainty, Paul regularly uses the Roman provincial names. This practice, then, may be said to constitute the rule.

It has been countered by others again, *e.g.,* by Schürer, that a general linguistic practice obtained, according to which the term Galatia included also the territories of Pisidia and Lycaonia. But later researches, among others those of Ramsay, have demonstrated the inaccuracy of this contention. Consider, *e.g.,* the documented article of J. Weiss in HRE, 10, 1901, page 556. There it is demonstrated that not only such writers as Ptolemy, Tacitus, and Pliny referred to the whole complex of territories belonging to the province by means of the comprehensive term Galatia, but also that the inscriptions, from which the linguistic practice of the time comes into clearer view, employ the name Galatia to refer to the Roman province. The inscription found at Iconium, for instance, is but one example of it. In this connection it is relevant also to refer to 1 Peter 1, where Galatia all but certainly refers not merely to the territory but to the whole province of that name. True, there are also some pieces of evidence, in the form of inscriptions, which point in the other direction. In any event, however, so much is certain that, alongside of the official legal practice, the contemporary popular usage also employed the term Galatia for designating the whole provincial unit. On this count, then, no serious objection can be raised to the South Galatian view.

(2) A second argument in favor of the South Galatian theory is that the familiarity with and the grasp of Jewish religion which is assumed in the letter (*cf.* Introduction,

24

III) seems to suit the South Galatian churches better. These churches, as is abundantly evident from Acts 13:14, 43 ff. and 14:1-7, 19, were in more continuous contact with Jews than were the North Galatian Celts, who for the most part lived their own life and probably were less familiar, therefore, with the Jewish law and the Jewish allegories (4:21-31). To this it has been objected that the churches of Iconium and Antioch, what with their better knowledge of Jewish thought, would not, so it would seem, permit themselves to be suddenly talked out of position by itinerant Jews from Jerusalem (Gal. 1:6). It might be supposed, the argument is, that the Jewish heretical teachers could look for more success in churches made up almost entirely of Gentiles. However, it appears from Acts 13:50 and 14:2, 4, and 19 that the Jewish influence bent on drawing the Gentiles away from Paul was very great at Antioch, Iconium, and Lystra. A Judaizing trend, therefore, which, so to speak, offered a compromise between Judaism and Christianity, definitely found many a point of contact in these areas. Important in this connection, too, is the fact that in Acts 16:1-5 the cities of Lystra, Derbe, and Iconium are named as precisely the places to which Paul transmitted the regulations of the apostolic conference. This does not have to imply, of course, that he said nothing about those regulations at other places, but it does go to show that in these cities especially the problem of Judaism called for attention — a circumstance which argues for susceptibility rather than immunity to Judaistic heresies.

It should be pointed out, too, that on the basis of the North Galatian theory, one could hardly appeal to unfamiliarity with the Jewish religion on the part of the inhabitants of the territory of Galatia, and thence to infer that Jews would naturally have found these people an easy prey to their designs. For the fact is precisely that the letter assumes a more intimate familiarity on the part of its readers with Jewish thought than, as we see it, could reasonably be expected in churches made up almost exclusively of native Gentiles.

(3) Another important basis for the great appeal of the South Galatian hypothesis is the fact that in Acts 13, 14, and 16 we get a full account of the establishment and career of the churches in the south, whereas we have only scant and problematical data (in Acts 16:6 and 18:23) concerning Paul's labors in the North Galatian area. In reply it is said that this *argumentum e silentio* can have little significance in this case, inasmuch as the Acts by no means offer a comprehensive report on Paul's missionary activities. For example, when Paul was working at Ephesus (Acts 19) a good deal took place, according to 2 Corinthians, between him and the church at Corinth of which we read nothing in the Acts. Besides, the Acts do not mention the founding of the church at Rome. Hence, too, and quite justly, it is regarded as very difficult to judge of the greater or lesser importance of the churches of that time. In view, however, of the generally accepted early date of the letter, the churches of North Galatia would, if at all, have been founded on Paul's so-called second and third missionary journeys. And since the Acts generally give us a clear, if sometimes a short, account of the founding of churches on Paul's journeys, it would have been regarded as remarkable that not a word is said there about the formation of churches in the North Galatian region. All we get from Acts 16:6 is that on his second missionary journey Paul and his co-workers went through the territory of Phrygia and Galatia; and from Acts 18:23 we learn again that, proceeding from Antioch, he went through Galatia and Phrygia in order, and this time with the addendum: "establishing the disciples." If both of these references are to one and the same Galatian region, and more specifically to the North Galatian territory, we should have to conclude from Acts 18:23 that Paul, on his travels through that area during his second missionary journey

(Acts 16:6), made some converts there (of the formation of churches nothing is said). That is all the Acts have to say about the winning of disciples (and about the formation of churches) in this territory. It should be clear, then, in view of such facts, that in identifying the churches of Gal. 1:2, we can get a better grip on what is known about the South Galatian churches than we can, from these scant reports, about North Galatia.

Others, following in the steps of W. Ramsay, go so far as to discredit every indication of Paul's having been in North Galatia (that is, in the territory). Such commentators judge that "the region of Galatia" of Acts 18:23 must be taken to refer, not to the North Galatian territory, but to the South Galatian province. They appeal to two considerations: *first,* to the tremendous detour which Paul would have had to make if, on his way to Ephesus, he had gone through North Galatia; and, *second,* to the expression "establishing all the brethren" when it has not become evident in what precedes that there were any disciples in North Galatia. That expression, these interpreters feel, would seem much more naturally applicable to the churches at Derbe, Lystra, and the rest, in the southern part of the province of Galatia. Such a view of the matter is the more attractive because we do not get the impression from Acts 16:6 that Paul travelled and worked in the territory of Galatia to such an extent that a later trip, like that reported in Acts 18:23, would be necessary.

A closer look at Acts 16:1-8 seems in order. Verses 1 to 5 are devoted to the journey which Paul and his fellows had made through the cities of Lystra, Derbe, and the rest. Then comes verse 6 with its report: "And they went through the regions of Phrygia and Galatia." Some have sought to construe this passage as a recapitulation of the journey through South Galatia. There would then be no reference at all to a trip through North Galatia. The context argues against this, however, for verse 6 plainly speaks of a continuation of the journey — a journey, moreover, which, as is suggested also by the reference to Phrygia, is moving in a northwestern and northern direction. That leaves us, however, with the very difficult question of what is meant by the phrase, "the region of . . . Galatia." If we construe it to mean the North Galatian territory and its cities, we shall have to accept the idea that Paul here swerved off to the east in a detour of a few hundred miles, preached the gospel there, and then came back to his point of origin in order to continue in the direction originally taken, namely, towards Bithynia. To read all this into the natural chronicle of the travelogue seems to us a bit far-fetched. If, then, we are compelled to interpret "the region of Galatia" as a reference to the North Galatian territory, and to this the context certainly seems to point, we need, presumably, be saying nothing more than that Paul and his party proceeded from Antioch in Pisidia through the country of Phrygia and Galatia while enroute to Bithynia in the north. This would not, however, be routing them through the much more easterly situated Galatian cities of Pessinus, Tavium, and Ancyra.

That Acts 18:23 must be taken to refer to this same territory seems to us subject to serious doubt. It is very difficult to accept the idea that in 18:23 Luke has Paul making that off-route circuit through Celtic Galatia in order (in the country between Phrygia and Galatia) to establish the brethren whom Luke has not previously mentioned. As we see it, there is nothing against accepting the thought that Luke, too, is speaking of Galatia in the broader sense so that in 16:6 it refers to the more northerly territory, and in 18:23 to the more southern parts.

In any event, it ought to be evident from all this that any founding and existence of churches in North Galatia can be inferred from the Acts with only very meager certainty.

(4) The further arguments that are advanced in defense of the so-called South Galatian hypothesis are, as we see it, of less importance. The fact, for instance, that Barnabas is mentioned three times in this letter is said to be subject to a natural explanation only if it is assumed that Barnabas was one of the co-founders of the South Galatian churches. Barnabas, however, was a well-known figure also outside the pale of churches which he himself had helped to establish (cf. 1 Cor. 9:6; Col. 4:10), although it must be acknowledged that he is nowhere in the focus of attention so much as in our letter (2:1, 9, 13).

Again, commentators have pointed out 1 Cor. 16:1, where Paul writes of the collection for the saints, adding that he gave the same order to the churches of Galatia. That the South Galatian churches are involved in that passage is thought to be confirmed by Acts 20:4, where the names of those are mentioned who were delegated, along with Paul, to carry the contributions. Among them are the names of Gaius from Derbe and of Timothy from Lystra. This argument, too, when taken in connection with other data that we have, is not without significance. All the same, it remains impossible, on the basis of so few facts, to reconstruct what is probably a much more complicated historical situation.

If one were to ask, now, what may be pleaded against the South Galatian hypothesis and what in favor of the North Galatian one, our reply would be that such is of even less importance.

(a) It is maintained that Gal. 4:13 is hard to harmonize with the account of Acts 13 and 14. Against this contention, two considerations are in order. *First,* that of all Paul's experiences such as he sums up in 2 Cor. 11:24 ff., only a few are reported by Luke in the Acts. Hence any silence on Luke's part about an illness which Paul had en route to South Galatia can hardly be taken as evidence that Gal. 4:13 is in conflict with the South Galatian theory.

Second, it is not necessary to hold that the "infirmity of the flesh" spoken of in Gal. 4:13 was necessarily an illness. As we see it, that infirmity may have been the physical suffering and exhaustion which accrued to Paul en route in the form of molestation at Antioch (Acts 13:50), and of stoning at Lystra (14:19). That last stoning was so severe that it was thought Paul had died as a consequence. Moreover, Acts 14:20 speaks of the loving care which the believers tendered Paul; and the same situation seems to have obtained at Derbe to which he escaped. Hence, all the conjectures about the significance of Paul's "illness" are probably superfluous, and Gal. 4:13 can best be explained in correspondence with the known facts of Acts 13 and 14. If this be true, the "infirmity of the flesh" is not an argument against but much more probably an argument for the South Galatian hypothesis.

(b) In the churches to which this letter is addressed, so it is argued, there were practically no Jews at all (5:2; 6:12). On the other hand, however, there were Jews in the churches at Antioch, Iconium, Lystra, and Derbe; at Iconium there were quite a few (Acts 14:1), and perhaps also at Antioch (Acts 13:43). Concerning that, this must be said first of all: that it is hard to tell whether the number of Jews who at first believed, even though at some places that was a considerable number, could maintain themselves after what the enemies did to counteract Paul's work in those very places (*cf.* Acts 13:45, 46; 14:2, 4). And next, this can be said: even though in this letter the readers are, in the main, thought of as Gentile-Christians, this need nowhere be taken so absolutely as to exclude the presence of a number of Jewish-Christians (*cf.* Introduction, II).

We conclude: a positive decision is not possible in this matter. The choice is not a simple one, especially because the authorities on the historical and archaeological particulars sometimes express differing opinions. As we see it, the evidence, on the basis of which the case must be made out, points to South rather than to North Galatia. Our letter is to be regarded, then, as a pastoral missive sent by Paul to the churches whose establishment is described for us in Acts 13 and 14 — churches which Paul visited again after their founding (Acts 16). These churches were among the first that he formed. It is no wonder that in a special sense they retained his love and care, as these are revealed in the letter. That they were especially vulnerable to the Jewish danger, and therefore were easily affected by Judaizing influences, is evident from the account of their establishment, and has already been explained above. Further, everything points to a very cordial relationship between the apostle and the churches (*cf.* 4:12 ff).

V

The Date

In accepting the South Galatian hypothesis we arrive at an earlier date. On that basis the *terminus a quo* lies in Paul's second visit to these churches (*cf.* Acts 16:1-4; Gal. 4:13): that is, if we fix the year of the apostolic council in 48 or 49. Apparently the letter was written not long afterward (*cf.* 1:6), probably in Corinth, where the apostle stayed for a while during his second missionary journey. That would then be in 50 or 51. The letter would then be among the first, if not actually the first, of the letters of Paul preserved for us. This is the judgment also of Th. Zahn, in his *Einleitung in das N.T.*, I (3rd. edit.), 1924, page 138 ff., who goes on to point to the fact that Paul transmits no greetings from Timothy and Silas, who were both in a special sense known to the South Galatian churches. He deduces from this fact that the letter had been sent off before these co-workers had arrived in Corinth (*cf.* Acts 18:5).

There is also a point of view which places this letter before the apostolic council held at Jerusalem in 48. One of the strongest grounds for this view is that, as its adherents suppose, Paul's journey to Jerusalem mentioned in Gal. 2:1 is a different journey from the one to the apostolic conference mentioned in Acts 15. In short, the supporters of this view think that the facts of Galatians 2 and those of Acts 15 concerning this journey do not square with each other. Even Calvin had judged that Paul's journey of Gal. 2 was the so-called collection-journey (*cf.* Acts 11:30). Much later this view of the matter was taken over by others, *e.g.,* by V. Weber.[3] The Tübingen school (F. Chr. Baur), especially, gave this view further impetus. It held, on the basis of an alleged disparity between Acts 15 and Gal. 2, to a thoroughgoing opposition between a Judaizing-Petrine and an anti-Jewish-universalistic-Pauline Christianity — an opposition which came to light clearly enough in Gal. 2, but was unhistorically blurred in the Acts. Then others, who did not want to follow this Tübingen criticism, found a way of escape from it by maintaining that the historical event alluded to in Gal. 2 was a different event from the meeting of the apostles reported in Acts 15. One of the strongest proponents of this view was V. Weber, who devoted no fewer than three published studies to it. Not long ago J. de Zwaan was still following in his wake. Weber is convinced that the journey of Paul reported in Gal. 2 precedes the apostolic conference, and that therefore the date of the letter must also be fixed at a time before that conference. He appeals to the supposed incongruency between Gal. 2 and Acts 15 reported above, and does so for the following reasons, among others:

(a) If the apostolic conference is assumed to precede the writing of the letter to the Galatians, one must ask

[3] In his *Die Abfassung des Galaterbriefs vor dem Apostelkonzil* (1900) p. 347.

himself how it can be that a teaching so solemnly and definitively repudiated at Jerusalem can almost immediately be preached again in Galatia. *Answer*: Heresy has never been abruptly and suddenly subjugated by the pronouncements of the church. In his later letters, too, *e.g.*, in the one to the Philippians, Paul has to take up the cudgels against Judaism.

(b) Why does not Paul appeal simply to the pronouncements of the apostolic conference instead of entering newly upon profound argumentation about the freedom of the Gentiles from the ceremonial law? *Answer*: He had already communicated these pronouncements to the churches on his second journey (Acts 16:4). Hence, too, his marvelling at the fact that they have so quickly allowed themselves to be brought around to the heresy (Gal. 1:6). That in this letter he does not simply appeal to the utterances of the apostolic conference, but instead resorts to the resource of a new principial apology, that — in view of what he had communicated to them during the visit of Acts 16:4 — is to be explained by the nature of the situation. Besides Gal. 2 illuminates the decisions reached at Jerusalem, and can thus serve as a confirmation of what he has already communicated by word of mouth (see the Exposition).

(c) Why does not Paul appeal to the utterances of James and Peter at the apostolic conference (Acts 15), so as to make impossible all efforts of the heretical teachers to set up a contrast between him and them? *Answer*: In the presence of the Galatians Paul was not concerned solely to maintain his essential unanimity with Peter and James: he was concerned also to maintain his independence over against those apostles. Hence he is at pains to show that at Jerusalem he did not for a moment betray the position which he had independently taken right from the start, and that he had received the approval of Peter and James for his stand.

(d) How — if this letter follows the apostolic conference — is the attitude of Peter to be explained, as it is described in Gal. 2:11 ff.? *Answer*: Peter's weakness was not that he demanded the observation of the Jewish ceremonies on the part of the Gentiles, but rather that, later, when some had come from James to Antioch, Peter, being a Jew, separated himself from the Gentiles with whom he had at first mingled fraternally, in order himself, personally, to observe the Jewish ceremonies again. This had not been forbidden by the apostolic conference at Jerusalem. It is true that in so doing he was again making a distinction between Jewish Christians and Gentile Christians; and thus he was also indirectly forcing the Gentiles, in the event they wanted to sit at table with their Jewish brethren, to conduct themselves as Jews (Gal. 2:14). For that he was reprimanded by Paul. But that was something quite different from what had been dealt with at the apostolic conference (see also the Exposition, under Gal. 2:1).

The main objection to the hypothesis championed by Weber, and others, is however this: the supposition that Acts 15 and Gal. 2 refer to two different journeys runs into serious difficulties. And when one tries to identify the journey of Gal. 2 with that of Acts 11:30, one is confronted with a series of historical difficulties.[4] Weber felt this to be true himself. In a later study he is of the opinion that the journey of Gal. 2 should be identified with a still earlier one, not even named in the Acts. That, of course, takes us even further into the area of hypothesis. For the time being, therefore, we hold to the interpretation which has been powerfully defended against the Tübingen criticism by S. Greijdanus, among others, namely, that there is no insurmountable obstacle to an identification of

---

[4] Cf. Zahn, *Der Brief des Paulus an die Galaten,* 3rd edit. (1922) pp. 109-112, where these difficulties are indicated.

the journeys of Gal. 2 and Acts 15.[5] There is no need of Weber's hypothesis, even though various elements of uncertainty remain. (See also the Exposition).

VI

Authenticity

After the Tübingen school, as a result of the so-called disparity between the Acts and the Letter to the Galatians, chose for the authenticity of the second, and rejected the Book of the Acts as of little historical value, the so-called radical Dutch school came forward with its contrasting view of the solution required by the alleged unreconcilability of the two books. According to this school, the Book of the Acts was to be regarded as the older and more reliable, and the Epistle to the Galatians was to be thought of, not as coming from Paul, but from the second century, just as the other letters of Paul, four of which (Romans, Galatians, and 1 and 2 Corinthians) the Tübingen school had, after all, still regarded as authentic. And further arguments were employed in support of a second century origin for the letter; for example: its lofty Christology, which, it was assumed, could only have arisen at a later time; the logical position which Paul here takes over against the law of Moses, something allegedly quite unthinkable in that early period; the dependence of the letter upon later New Testament, extra-canonical, and even pagan writings.

This radical criticism which first doubted the authenticity of the letter to the Galatians (Evanson, 1792), then denied its genuineness altogether (Bruno Bauer, 1850), was continued especially in The Netherlands, namely, by Loman, Pierson, Naber, van Manen, and, following in their

---

[5] Cf. S. Greijdanus, *Is Handelingen ix (met 22 en 26) in tegenspraak met Galaten 1, 2 ?* (1935).

steps, by the Swiss Steck. Others, for whom such radical criticism went too far, claimed that the letter was a combination of an original Pauline text with insertions and interpolations of a much later date. Among such, acting in imitation of Weiss, were Baljon, Cramer, Völter, and others.

Gradually, however, this whole body of criticism has more and more been brought to silence. It is possible now to say that there is not a single letter that is so generally regarded as authentic as is Paul's letter to the Galatians. This hypercriticism has come to be recognized in its arbitrariness and in the unsoundness of its point of departure, and its arguments have proved worthless. It arises out of a view of Christianity and its development which has proved quite unsound. Such is true, for example, of the contrast between a Pauline and a Petrine Christianity, of the later development of a so-called transcendental Christology, and the like. The arbitrariness of the endless interpolation theories, too, has gradually come to be recognized, and students have developed an eye again for the thoroughly personal and vital quality of the letter. It bears, so to speak, the mark of its genuineness on its forehead.

EXPOSITION

THE EPISTLE OF PAUL TO THE CHURCHES OF GALATIA

CHAPTER I

THE SALUTATION

1:1-5

1 Paul, an apostle (not from men, neither through man, but through Jesus Christ, and God the Father, who raised him from the dead),

2 and all the brethren that are with me, unto the churches of Galatia:

3 Grace to you and peace from God the Father, and our Lord Jesus Christ,

4 who gave himself for our sins, that he might deliver us out of this present evil world, according to the will of our God and Father:

5 to whom *be* the glory for ever and ever. Amen.

The *exordium* of this letter contains the three customary elements which were found at the beginning of an ancient letter: namely, the announcement of the writer, the designation of the readers, and the opening salutation. Not that in practice such an *exordium* need take on a stereotyped quality. Rather, it is oriented to the readers and to the particular purpose of the letter. This is very evident in the letter to the Galatians. The way in which Paul designates himself (verse 1) immediately places the emphasis on his divine calling, something that in the sequel proves to be one of the main themes of the letter. The designation of the readers (verse 2) is uncommonly short, something, in turn, that is in keeping with the tense relationships between Paul and the churches of Galatia. The salutation (verses 3 and 4) describes the grace of God in such a way that the intelligent reader will immediately detect from the centrality of the work of Christ in it what the decision must be in the big issue which dominates the letter. *Semina sparguntur tractationis* (Bengel).

1 Together with his name, Paul immediately thrusts his apostleship into the foreground, and he does it with penetrating, antithetical force. An *apostle*[1] is a minister plenipotentiary (*cf.* John 20:21 ff.). The source of his ambassadorship is first indicated negatively: *not from men, neither through man*.[2] He does this certainly as defense against his challengers in the churches of Galatia, who have attacked or undermined his authority. Over against them the apostle lays claim to having been directly called through[3] Christ. He refers in that connection to Christ the Lord according to His human manifestation and according to His office. Both had been revealed to Paul in his calling by Christ (*cf.* 1 Cor. 9:1). The directly appended *and God the Father*[4] announces that Paul's calling of Christ was simultaneously a calling of God. The one is not to be separated from the other. Being called of

---

[1] The word is used in the first place for the twelve disciples, whom Jesus also calls apostles (Luke 6:13). At other places in the New Testament, however, it is also applied to other persons who carried out a mission in the proclamation of the gospel (*cf.* Acts 14:4, 14, Gal. 1:19, and Rom. 16:7). See also the exposition of 1:19.

[2] There is no article for the word in the Greek. The accent is on the human as such, on man. The word *from* (ἀπό) designates in the main the derivation and origin. These are not men (notice the plural!), whoever and wherever they may be. The word *through* (διά) points rather to the medium. Then follows *man*, the singular form this time, because a single human being could serve as that medium. The expression is not in conflict with such passages as Acts 9:17 and 13:2. Christ Himself had appeared to Paul (Acts 9:5, 6; *cf.* 22:8). Ananias simply informed him what he had to do in carrying out Christ's commission (*cf.* Acts 22:8).

[3] Here the *through* (διά) has not merely an instrumental, but also a causative significance, in which the means can be regarded as being understood. When used for God and for Christ διά can have a richer content than ἀπό.

[4] The original is Θεοῦ πατρός, without the intervening καί (*cf.* verse 5). God's fatherhood is part and parcel of His divine being. His existence is the source of all life.

God gives expression to the profoundest and most essential nature of the calling. Divine authority stands behind it. Paul is God's own and special ambassador. The Galatians must understand that! And the addition, *who raised him from the dead,* reinforces still more the connection between Christ and the Father, and between both of these and Paul's calling. What the readers must do first of all is to grasp the divine and the glorious in Christ's work, for the Judaizers have blurred these things. And now, think of it, of that Christ, raised of God, Paul is the apostle! So it was, and therefore, although he was not a disciple of Jesus like the others, he could, nevertheless, after Jesus' death, be sent of Him. And so his mission and his full authority were determined by the glory of the One who sent him.

2 By the *brethren* mentioned here Paul's co-workers are probably meant, and not the believers at the place where he wrote (*cf.* Phil. 4:21-22). Who these co-workers were cannot be ascertained. One's idea of that depends upon one's idea of the place at which the letter was written (see Introduction). These brethren are not named as fellow-authors but are nevertheless included in the address and salutation. Together with Paul they know the lay of the land, and reckon themselves co-responsible.[5] For the rest, there is neither here, nor in the whole letter, any allusion to reciprocal relationships. The atmosphere is too tense and business-like (*cf.,* for contrast, *e.g.,* Rom. 1:7; 1 Cor. 1:2; 2 Cor. 1:1; and Col. 1:2). Remarkable, too, is the plural: *the churches.* It pertains to the various local churches in the province (or the territory) of Galatia.[6] It is singular in verse 13.

---

[5] The rather emphatic *all* which modifies *the brethren* can, in this connection, refer to the positiveness and finality with which they supported Paul in his case against the churches of Galatia.

[6] Concerning the problem of whether the province or the territory (the South Galatian and the North Galatian hypotheses) is intended, see the Introduction.

3 This constitutes the salutation proper. *Grace*[7] and *peace*[8] give general expression to the reconciling relationship between God and His people and to the full salvation included in it. Here again is the reference to God *the Father* (*cf.* verse 1), this time to be thought of specifically as expressing His relation to the believers.[9] God is also a Father apart from this relationship (verse 1). His fatherhood cannot be explained by analogy with human fatherhood. But in Christ His fatherly disposition in a special sense goes out to the believers. Coming from the mouth of the fully authorized apostle of Christ, this salutation is not only a wish, but an efficient blessing given in

---

[7] We cannot be sure whether this *grace* (χάρις) was typical of the general Greek manner of greeting. As a rule, the salutation of a Greek letter uses χαίρειν rather than χάρις (*cf.* O. Roller, *Das Formular der paulinischen Briefe*, 1933, p. 61 ff.) It is quite possible, therefore, that the χάρις employed here and elsewhere represents an early Christian (or specifically Pauline?) mode of greeting, and that it was rather the Jewish form of greeting (שלום *peace*) which formed the point of contact in the frequent greetings of Paul's letters (*cf.* TWNT, II, p. 412 εἰρήνη). In any event, the word χάρις is used in the New Testament in a specific sense. In profane usage χάρις refers to something which arouses a person's joy or desire: beauty, for instance, or grace, or fame. Or, in the social relationship of a higher to a lower class or status, it means favor or approbation. In the New Testament, however, it refers to God's favor towards His people in Christ—a favor which rests on forgiveness, on reconciliation.

[8] In the Christian sense, εἰρήνη (which corresponds to the Hebrew שלום, also employed as a greeting) generally refers to the condition of well-being in which the whole world will share through Christ's coming (Luke 2:14). It can also be used in a restricted sense, and it then means the restored relationship between God and man in which the juridical element is in the foreground (*cf.* Rom. 5:1), or else the condition of inner peace, or soul's rest, which Christ grants through the Holy Spirit (*cf.* Rom. 15:13 and Phil. 4:7), or yet again the Christian peace present among people socially (*cf.* Rom. 14:17). The first meaning, designating the eschatological state of salvation, is the fundamental one.

[9] In some manuscripts, which have the reading καὶ κυρίου ἡμῶν instead of ἡμῶν καὶ κυρίου this is even more explicit.

42

the name of Christ (*cf.* Mark 5:34; Matt. 10:12 ff.; and John 14:27).

4 By way of exception to the usual pattern of the salutation, the apostle attaches a long description of the work of Christ to his mention of the name of Christ. This at once thrusts the purpose of the letter to the fore: the issue between Paul and the Galatians is the significance of Christ. It is He *who gave*[10] *himself for*[11] *our sins*. The active verb suggests the voluntariness, and the reflexive pronoun speaks of the personal and the total in His surrender (*cf.* Mark 10:45). It is above all Christ's death that the apostle chooses to stress. This death was necessary because of our sins: Christ's self-surrender had a reconciling significance. The idea is not at this point worked out in detail; the overture hints at the grand theme only in a general way. True, a particular phase of the purpose and effect of this self-surrender is designated: *that*[12] *he might deliver us out of this present*[18] *evil world*. This world[14] (which really means: world-period) is a world qualified by sin; the devil is its God (2 Cor. 4:4; *cf.* 1 Cor. 2:6, and Eph. 2:2). Hence, because of its sin, it will go to its doom. The purpose of the purging of sin through

---

[10] The participle τοῦ δόντος has a qualifying significance. Christ's self-surrender is not an historical deed merely; His whole being is characterized by *giving*.

[11] Some manuscripts have περί, others ὑπέρ, apparently without a difference in meaning (*cf.* Rom. 8:3 and 1 Cor. 15:3). In other passages, too, περί is used to designate the idea of reconciliation for sin (for example, in the LXX Ex. 32:20, Lev. 5:6, 6:26, and others).

[12] ὅπως: so that thus.

[18] Instead of the particle ἐνεστώς used with αἰών other places have ὁ αἰών οὗτος (*cf.* Rom. 12:2, 1 Cor. 1:20, 2:6, and other places). This is in distinction from ὁ αἰών μέλλων (*cf.* Eph. 1:2 and Mt. 12:32), and also from the coming (ἐπερχόμενοι) aeons (Eph. 2:7), after the judgment of the world, when there shall be the new heaven and the new earth.

[14] αἰών: period of time, world-period, world.

Christ is therefore also a redemption from this world as a doomed place (*cf.* Gen. 19:16 ff.). All the same this deliverance spoken of here has more than a local, eschatological significance. It consists also of a loosing of the saints from the sinful ties of this world, and of a liberation from the divine curse and wrath which rest on this world, so that for believers their share in the suffering and death of this world gets to have a different meaning (*cf.* Rom. 8:18, 35 ff.). And all this happens *according to the will*[15] of our *God and*[16] *Father.* He is the author of the reconciliation and redemption in Christ. His revealed will is the norm for it.

5   The doxology[17] here at the very beginning, followed by the stately confirmation of the *Amen!*, right from the start denominates the divine work of redemption as transcendent and beyond praise, high and lifted up above the realm of criticism and objection such as, at bottom, the churches of Galatia are directing against it. The doxology serves[18] not only to declare[19] that the heavenly glory is due to God, but also to summon men to join in with it and to conduct themselves accordingly.[20] The objectivity of God's

---

[15] What is intended by the *will* (θέλημα) is not God's counsel, but the will which issues from it: hence, command or commission. This *will* has been made known in Christ and has been fulfilled by Him in His redemptive work.

[16] καί has distinctive force here: Our God and *at the same time* our Father. God's wisdom and omnipotence as well as His fatherly disposition determine His will.

[17] δόξα in the New Testament (unlike its meaning in profane usage, where it refers to the subjective *sense,* and also to the *respect* accorded a person) often has the signification of what in the Old Testament is called the *kebod Jahwe:* the manifestation of the divine glory (*cf.* G. Kittel, *Die Religionsgeschichte und das Urchristentum,* 1932, pp. 82-85).

[18] The verb is missing. ἐστιν as well as εἴη is involved.

[19] ἐστιν: compare 1 Peter 4:11, and the like.

[20] εἴη: compare Psalm 112:2 (LXX).

glory is, however, the dominant emphasis, as can be seen also from the *for ever and ever.*[21] For comment on the *Amen,* see the exposition of 6:18.

---

[21] The εἰς τοὺς αἰῶνας τῶν αἰώνων really applies a time limitation to God. Accordingly the idea is here indicated in the plural and is repeated, in order to signify the infinitely enduring: *unto eternity.*

NO OTHER GOSPEL

1:6-9

6 I marvel that ye are so quickly removing from him that
called you in the grace of Christ[1] unto a different gospel;

7 which is not another *gospel*: only there are some that
trouble you, and would pervert the gospel of Christ.

8 But though we, or an angel from heaven, should preach
unto you any gospel other than that which we preached
unto you, let him be anathema.

9 As we have said before, so say I now again, If any man
preacheth unto you any gospel other than that which ye
received, let him be anathema.

Right at the beginning the apostle raises the issue of
the threatening apostacy of the churches of Galatia. It is
the matter with which his heart is full. There is no occasion to express gratitude for the loyalty of the churches.
For an expression of interest in the fortunes and the
struggle of those churches, this is not the place. The painful and dangerous alienation between the apostle and the
churches must be discussed forthwith and headon.

6 The expression of wonder with which the apostle
makes his contact with the readers has in it something painful, almost ironical. An incredible right-about-face has
taken place among them in which the whole gospel is at
stake. And that so *quickly* after they had accepted the

---

[1] Although this translation can appeal to the most textual sources,
the rendering is nevertheless uncertain. For there is also a very old
original which lacks the Χριστοῦ (thus P⁴⁶G, Marc. Tert.) Because
the inclusion of Χρ' makes for easier explanation than the omission
of it, one gives his preference to this rendering. This implies a sort
of difference, too, for the exegesis.

gospel.[2] True, this about-face gets its impetus from others; but they, the Galatians, are not purely passive in the matter either: they are allowing themselves to be drawn away, and this process is now in full swing. It is all the more incredible and culpable when one marks the *him that called* them. This *him* refers not merely to the proclaimer of the Gospel, Paul himself, but to God also. So much can be inferred from the term *called,* the technical term for the divine activity with the gospel (*cf.* Rom. 8:30; 9:12, 24; 1 Cor. 1:9, and others). This at the same time implies something about the nature of this calling. As divine calling it is full of power and effect (*cf.* Rom. 11:29), never a single, innocent invitation, carrying no obligation with it. All the same, it does not realise itself outside the pale of human responsibility, but places precisely those who pay no attention[3] to this calling in a highly culpable position.[4] Thus the apostle confronts his readers with the seriousness of the reversal that is materializing itself among them. The words *in the grace of Christ* must be interpreted as referring to the purpose[5] of the calling; thus the contrast with the legalism of the Judaizers comes into the clearest light.

---

[2] This *quickly* may also be taken to refer to the short time that has elapsed since Paul's last visit to the Galatians (*cf.* verse 9). It seems better to us, however, to regard the contrast as absolute, that is, as the contrast between a glorious beginning and what now threatens to take place. So the *quickly* takes on even profounder meaning.

[3] Compare Isaiah 50:2 (LXX): ἐκάλεσα καὶ οὐκ ἦν ὁ ὑπακούων.

[4] All the same, the relationship between the divine calling by whose *efficacia* alone the sinner can come to faith and the human obstinacy which resists it remains a mystery for us (*cf.* Matt. 22:14). Reformed theology distinguishes with reference to the result between *vocatio interna* and *vocatio externa.*

[5] More than once καλέω is connected with ἐν in the sense of εἰς (*Cf.* 1 Cor. 7:15, Eph. 4:4, and 1 Thess. 4:7 in connection with 2 Thess. 2:14). One can, however, also regard the ἐν as having instrumental force: *through,* as in Rom. 3:24, and at other places, where the redemption through grace is spoken of. In connection, however, with the immediately following εἰς ἕτερον εὐαγγέλιον, the χάρις would seem to point to purpose (*Cf. Bl.-Debr.,* par. 218).

And when, finally, the apostle speaks of *a different gospel,* he d es so in a distinctive manner.[6] He is alluding to the here: y of those who want to deflect the Galatians from the one and only gospel. And so he immediately dismisses the thou ht that he might have implied that the other teaching desei ved the name of gospel (verse 7).

7 But there is no such thing as another[7] gospel. There are only[8] certain persons[9] who constantly busy themselves[10]

---

[6] That is to say, *Gospel* is not to be regarded as a general class name. It is a term which in an exclusive sense refers to the salvation that has appeared in Christ. The idea has its roots in the Old Testament, especially in the prophecies of Isaiah 40 ff. (in which we read of the messenger of joy announcing the dawn of salvation: Isa. 52:7), not in Hellenism (*cf.* J. Schniewind, *Euangelion,* I, 1927, and TWNT, II, p. 705 ff.).

[7] This time it is ἄλλο and not ἕτερον as in verse 6. On the basis of this shift of words, scholars have launched upon all sorts of involved conceptions of the words ὅ οὐκ ἔστιν ἄλλο. Now it is true that ἕτερος originally means: the other, or second, of two; and ἄλλος originally means: another of several. But it is very hard to see what this distinction can mean here. Besides, all kinds of contamination creep into the Koine (*cf., e.g.,* Matt. 5:39). Sometimes both words are used in one and the same connection, but, it would seem, solely for variation, and without significance (*cf.* 2 Cor. 11:4 and 1 Cor. 12:9 ff.). For this reason, also, it seems to us quite unnecessary to hold that what Paul wishes to say here is that the other gospel (in the *enumerative* sense), from which the Galatians were in process of turning away, could be no other gospel (in the *qualitative* sense) (*cf.* 2 Cor. 11:4). Rather, what Paul wants to do at this point is to reject the whole idea of another gospel as being absurd. True, he used the word himself in verse 6, but as a matter of fact, he means to say, such another gospel does not exist (ἔστιν). Further, ἄλλο seems to have a kind of pleonastic significance here, serving to introduce εἰ μή (*cf. nihil aliud nisi*). So, also, *Bl.-Debr.,* par. 306, 4.

[8] The εἰ μή which introduces the clause makes it limit what went before: *unless, except.* Sometimes it has the meaning of a simple contrast: *but* (*cf. Bl.-Debr.,* par. 376, 488, 8). It can also, however, be somewhat ironically interpreted: such another gospel does not exist except in the imaginations of those who are bringing confusion upon you.

[9] The original τινες is not without disdain.

[10] The original of the verb is progressive present: are troubling.

in their effort to confuse the Galatians. To *trouble* means, in this connection, to bring about spiritual schism and an obscuration of the insight of faith (*cf.* 5:10). They were doing this, as becomes evident in more detail later, by trying to lay down a different basis for salvation, or, at least by calling the gospel preached by Paul an inadequate one. Those who propagated this are denominated in the plural here. They apparently constituted a group of persons who, from the outside, and also probably under alien influence, resisted Paul's preaching. Their intent[11] was nothing less than to overturn the gospel that had Christ as its content[12] and to live out an opposing principle. This happens when the cross of Christ is no longer recognized in its all-sufficiency (*cf.* 5:2 ff.). Then the gospel is turned upside-down and robbed of its strength.

8 By means of a sharp turn[13] in the course of his argument, the apostle next puts up a hypothetical case: that not certain quite unqualified persons merely (such as they of verse 7), but he himself,[14] or even an angel from heaven,[15] were to preach[16] another[17] gospel from the one he had brought them. Then the curse[18] of God would have

---

[11] θέλοντες: with the deliberately intended meaning: not unconsciously or unwittingly.

[12] Although Christ also is and remains the subject of the preaching (*cf.* Eph. 4:11), the genitive in this connection means: the gospel *concerning* Christ (*Cf.* Mark 1:1, Rom. 15:19, 2 Cor. 4:5).

[13] 'Ἀλλὰ καὶ ἐάν: but even **though**.

[14] *We:* literary plural: perhaps the apostle is also thinking of his co-workers (verse 2).

[15] The *from heaven* modifies *an angel,* not *preached.* The prepositional phrase serves to enhance the glory of the angel. It is incredible that an angel should come from heaven with such a message.

[16] The verb comes to us in the conditional aorist, as well as in the indicative and the present conditional forms. In the Koine the distinction is not sharply maintained, even for conditional situations.

[17] παρ' ὅ: in departure from, in opposition to.

to be pronounced upon him or upon such an angel. To this extent the truth of the gospel transcends all else in importance, and to this extent that man is culpable who, in preaching it, modifies it on his own authority. On the one hand, this gives expression to how deeply conscious the apostle was of the divine truth of the gospel he preached and of his apostolic authority; on the other, it gives expression to how entirely subjected as a person he wanted to be to this truth and to the commission assigned him. The same would be true even for an angel from heaven. And not only is the truth more than the highest-ranking minister of God, but as the *gospel* — which constitutes the norm of the divine redemption in the world — it is so holy that anyone who independently modifies it brings the curse of God down upon his head.[19] This, then, is something the Galatians can pause to consider, now that they have given place in their midst to "another" gospel, preached not by Paul, nor by an angel, but by a number of unauthorized persons.

9 The apostle had[20] previously already[21] made such a statement. The Galatians, therefore, are well aware of the gravity under which the gospel had been preached to them. The fact that the apostle had earlier issued such a

---

[18] *Anathema* (ἀνάθεμα) is a cognate of ἀνάθημα, and originally meant something that is offered or dedicated to the deity or to God (*cf.* Luke 21:5). Later it also meant: something yielded up to the wrath of God, surrendered to the curse of God. It is in this last sense that ἀνάθεμα is usually used (so in the New Testament: Rom. 9:3, 1 Cor. 12:3, 16:22; *cf.* Acts 23:12, 21). This curse of excommunication is not to be thought of in the sense of ecclesiastical discipline—after all, an angel, too, is hypothetically involved —but as a general curse.

[19] ἔστω: *let him be:* not a wish merely, but a solemn affirmation of what certainly shall be.

[20] The force of the *have said* is that of the perfect: once and for all. It holds for the present too.

[21] Presumably the *said before* refers to an earlier visit, not to the preceding clause, inasmuch as the *now* (ἄρτι) can hardly designate a period of time other than that of verse 8.

warning indicates that he knew the fatal danger involved in falsifying the gospel. He had had experience of it before (see below). Now he is no longer speaking, as in verse 8, in terms of future supposition but rather of the present concrete situation.[22] The threat of the overthrow of the gospel confronts them directly here.[23] That gives the curse which is called down upon such falsification high concreteness and reality. The apostle is not appalled into timidity in applying that curse concretely. This should induce the readers who know better[24] to keep themselves far from the threatening heresy. It has been justly observed that Paul, who is tolerant with regard to opposition is not so in objective matters of fact.

---

[22] εἰ with the indicative as against ἐάν with the subjunctive.

[23] The force of *any man* (τις) is general, it is true, but plainly refers to the τινες of verse 7.

[24] The gospel had not merely been preached to them; they had *received* it, appropriated it as their own also.

PART ONE

Paul's Defense of His Apostolic Qualifications

1:10-2:21

In connection with the foregoing, Paul now begins to defend his apostolic authority against the attacks directed upon it. This defense continues to the end of Chapter 2, although in 2:15-21 the objective antithesis of the gospel itself begins to come to expression also. This portion, therefore, constitutes the transition to Chapter 3, in which the opposition between *the works of the law* and *faith in Christ* is the sharply focussed issue at stake. From 1:10 to 2:21 the apostle deals directly and primarily with his credentials as an apostle. He approaches this matter from more than one point of view. The transition to the discussion of this is constituted by verses 10 and 11.

THE GOSPEL ACCORDING TO MAN

1:10,11

10 For am I now seeking the favor of men, or of God? or am I striving to please men? if I were still pleasing men, I should not be a servant of Christ.

11 For I make known to you, brethren, as touching the gospel which was preached by me, that it is not after man.

10 The rhetorical question is apparently asked in response to the proffered charge that Paul had been trying to play up to the people in order to gain effect. Considering the nature of the opposition, we conclude the charge was made against Paul in the matter of his maintaining Gentile freedom from the Jewish law over against the militant Judaizers. In this circumstance then his opponents could find a pretense ready at hand for charging that Paul was playing up to the popular wish to "let down the bars" of responsible conduct. Over against this Paul puts the question whether they would care to charge this against him *now*[1] also, that is, now that he has in the preceding verses spoken as he has.[2] There he certainly was not using language nicely calculated to give offense to no one.[3] The question, consequently, is not without its irony. True, the charge probably took its point of departure from Paul's

---

[1] Ἄρτι with accent at the beginning: *now*, that is, now that I pronounce this judgment (of verses 8 and 9).

[2] The question is first of all one which shows reason or cause (γάρ): one can make out from it why the apostle dared speak as unequivocally as he did. Further, the question invites the attention to something new: Paul's apostolic independence.

[3] Always *men*, generic man, without the article: anyone, whoever it might be. The challengers meant the Gentiles by it. Paul by his independent attitude over against the heretical teachers, proves that he is currying neither their favor, nor that of people in general.

attitude towards the law. And his defense now leans upon a robust maintenance of his previously proclaimed gospel. And that should be enough to prove, consequently, that Paul was not out to win people by telling them what they like to hear.[4] Besides, his preaching of this gospel had brought him into sharp conflict with others. It was therefore the motive of obedience to God[5] that prompted him to speak as he had spoken. But for this he would not have taken so radically thoroughgoing a position. The last part of the sentence[6] confirms all this by pointing to the fact that human desire and the service of Christ are incompatible. This is so not merely on the basis of the general rule of Matt. 6:24, but especially also because of the nature of the service of Christ. The service of Christ goes straight against the grain of what people naturally love to hear (cf. 5:11 and 6:12); the service of Christ demands precisely a readiness to surrender everything for His sake, and most particularly this favor of men.

11 The words, For I make known to you, brethren, suggest something remarkable and impressive. They indicate that the readers do not yet know, or no longer know, the truth that is to follow,[7] although they might well have

---

[4] First we have πείθω, then ἀρέσκω. The first must be construed in agreement with the second, and so the force of the statement becomes: to gain someone for one's self by playing up to what he wants. The tense suggests a continuing habit, typical of the agent.

[5] The added ἢ τὸν Θεόν as an alternative has something gratifying in it. That Paul's way of doing aimed at quite the opposite of what the plaintiffs are charging him with is thus sharply focussed upon the attention.

[6] After the rhetorical question, comes a condition: εἰ...ἤρεσκον The adverbial still points not so much to details of Paul's earlier life as to the inclination present in every man to ingratiate himself with others; hence "if I had not unlearnt it."

[7] The Greek construction is somewhat irregular, because the ὅτι does not precede but follows the τὸ εὐαγγέλιον... All the same, the logical object of γνωρίζω is not the noun τὸ εὐαγγέλιον, but the objective clause, namely, that it is not after men (cf. verse 13). Hence the translation: as touching the gospel . . .

known and reflected on it.   Paul, so to speak, has to begin
again at the very beginning.   Although the tone is friendly,
and although the vocative *brethren* — used sparingly in
this letter — first appears in this connection, this formal
announcement nevertheless has something in it that puts
to shame.   If they did not yet know that the gospel which
the apostle had preached[8] to them was not after men,[9] then
they had better let themselves be told this truth in a most
formal manner, once and for all.

---

[8] The words *which was preached by me* communicate two things:
that the Galatians had heard it and might thus have known it; and
that the apostle is taking no responsibility for what others had
eventually preached to them as gospel.

[9] The force of the *not after men* is that what Paul preached to
them is not determined by human approbation, taste, or preference.

PAUL, TOO, ONCE AN ENEMY OF THE GOSPEL

1:12-14

12 For neither did I receive it from man, nor was I taught it, but *it came to me* through revelation of Jesus Christ.

13 For ye have heard of my manner of life in time past in the Jews' religion, how that beyond measure I persecuted the church of God, and made havoc of it:

14 and I advanced in the Jews' religion beyond many of mine own age among my countrymen, being more exceedingly zealous for the traditions of my fathers.

12 The apostle now begins speaking about his own past, in order the better to demonstrate the nature of the gospel and of his own apostolic qualifications and independence. The historical data are not to be thought of as a sort of partial autobiography, but rather from the objective point of view of the issue at stake in this discussion. Verse 12 constitutes a transition. What is said in verse 11 can be understood partly in terms of the fact that Paul did not receive the gospel he preached from men,[1] nor by tradition,[2] nor by instruction,[3] but by revelation.[4] For the

---

[1] Presumably the οὐδέ in the first place modifies the verb. Nevertheless, the ἐγώ which is expressly added, also gets some of the emphasis. Paul, too, required a revelation in order to appropriate the gospel.

[2] The παρέλαβον of the *did I receive* is the technical term for oral tradition, as it was exercised particularly also in the rabbinical schools and also was taught to the people.

[3] The *nor was I taught it* is a specific reference to academic instruction. In this connection, the immediately preceding *receive* is presumably to be taken as referring to the general, as distinguished from the school, tradition. The words *from man* modify also the *nor was I taught it*. Otherwise the ἐδιδάχθην would be too absolute, and the conclusion of the clause would be too loosely independent from the rest of the predication.

[4] In general, *revelation* (ἀποκάλυψις) means this: announcement

rest, the attention is called, not so much to the way in which Paul came in contact with the gospel (he does not place himself outside the pale of *Christian* tradition (*cf.* 1 Cor. 7:10, 11:23, and 15:3), as to the origin of the gospel. Nevertheless there is emphasis on the immediacy of Paul's calling to the gospel directly through[5] Christ. It had been a supernatural revelation, this by which he had become serviceable to Christ. The apostle is here plainly referring to the event at Damascus (Acts 9:3 ff.). There Christ had appeared to him. It does not necessarily follow, of course, that up to that moment Paul knew nothing about Jesus; but there he was persuaded of the objective divinity and truth of the Messiah confessed by the church (*cf.* verse 13).

13 This verse carries us still farther into Paul's past, and speaks of his activity against the church of Christ before his conversion. His narration of this is designed to drive home the more tellingly that his apostleship rests upon God's own intervention. In this connection, Paul makes his appeal to what the Galatians themselves had heard concerning him, whether from Paul himself, from others, or, as is probable, from both (*cf.* 1 Cor. 15:9, 1 Tim. 1:12 ff., and Phil. 3:5 ff.). First the apostle gives a general designation of this past as *my manner of life[6] in time past in*

---

from God's side of what lies beyond human reach. It assumes, often, not merely a manifestation, a disclosing in the objective sense, but also an influencing of the human spirit in such a way that it can distinguish the divine revelation as being such (*cf.* Mt. 16:17). In this verse it means not merely a change that has invaded and seized upon Paul's mind, but also and primarily the objective intervention of Christ. In other places, Paul puts this event on the same level of fact as the appearances of the Risen One (1 Cor. 9:1 and 15:8).

---

[5] The genitive 'Ιησοῦ Χριστοῦ is here to be regarded as constituting the general subject (compare the Exposition of verse 16).

[6] The ἀναστροφήν refers to his ethical conduct.

the Jews' religion,[7] then a more specific[8] reference to his extraordinary persecution of the church of God and to his devastation[9] of it. We are to think of what is told us in Acts 8:1 ff., 9:1 ff. and 13 ff., 22:4 ff., and 16:9 ff. The term *church* is not to be thought of in the regional sense of verse 2, but in a general sense.[10] By calling it *the church of God,* the apostle makes the frightfulness of his former activity the more manifest. At the same time, the phrase communicates the idea that the believers in Christ are the continuation of Israel as the people chosen of God.[11] Indirectly this implies that the criterion for belonging to the people of God lies in faith and in nothing else.

---

[7] The Ἰουδαϊσμῷ can mean both the objective Jewish life and work and the subjective embodiment of living as a Jew. Here, very probably, the objective sense obtains: my performance when I still belonged to the Jewish communion and was committed to the Jewish life-view.

[8] The objective clause, which is introduced by ὅτι, announces what Paul really means to say. See, for this construction, verse 11 also.

[9] The imperfect tenses here stress the continuing and the intensive character of the persecution and the making havoc; the form is ἐπόρθουν (for which, in some manuscripts, the more ordinary ἐπολέμουν is given), *de conatu,* although the effort partly succeeded: hence the translation: *to make havoc of.* The verb really means *to devastate* or *lay waste,* and is also applied to persons.

[10] Concerning the relationship of these two it can be said that the local church is not merely a sub-division of the general ekklesia. The basic thought is rather that the total church represents itself in each local church, however small it may be. On the one hand, accordingly, the existence of the local church is not dependent upon the ekklesia in general; and, on the other hand, there is no room for congregational self-direction and individualism. Each church is ekklesia only and truly in so far as it represents the church of God in the general and ideal sense of the word (*cf.* also K. L. Schmidt, TWNT, III, pp. 504, 508, and elsewhere).

[11] The word *ekklesia* is also used to designate a profane popular assembly in the Hellenistic world (*cf.* Acts 19:32, 39 ff.). Whether the word is also used in a non-Christian cultic sense cannot be ascertained, but it is untenable that Paul would have appropriated such a use for designating the church of God. For ἐκκλησία is continuously used in LXX as the translation of *kahal,* particularly, too, in the combination *kehal Jahwe,* designating the theocratic popular

14 Besides being a persecutor of the church, Paul had been a fanatic zealot for the Jewish institutions. This, too, can serve to demonstrate once more how little his current zeal for Christ is the result of human deliberation. More and more meticulously he had worked himself into and made the Jewish religion and prescriptions his own[12] and had accommodated his conduct to them. He passed his contemporaries[13] by, as though in competition with them. His zeal[14] converged particularly upon *the tradition of (his) fathers.* This *tradition* refers to the so-called *halacha,* the compilation of ethical and other rules which took their point of departure from the Torah, and, by all sorts of addition and casuistical glossing, finally constituted a regimen for the whole of life (*cf.* Matt. 5:21 ff., 15:2, and 23:2 ff.).

---

assembly of Israel, and thus generally the Old Testament people of God. By now using the nomenclature *ekklesia of God* in distinction from Judaism, these two are already being denominated two entirely different communions. The ekklesia of God, although coming up out of, and constituting a unity with, the true, Old Testament people of God, is now an independent magnitude, standing next to and over against Jewry in the external sense of that word.

---

[12] προέκοπτον: imperfect tense, as above; the force of the *advanced* is to hew out a path as a pioneer.

[13] The ἐν τῷ γένει μου has the specific connotation: *of my people* (*cf.* Phil. 3:5).

[14] The *zealous* is not to be construed in a political sense (*cf.* Luke 6:15 and Acts 1:13) but as religious ardor (*cf.* what follows).

PAUL INDEPENDENT OF MEN IN HIS APOSTOLIC COMMISSION

1:15-17

15 But[1] when it was the good pleasure of God,[2] who separated me, *even* from my mother's womb, and called me through his grace,

16 to reveal his Son in me, that I might preach him among the Gentiles; straightway I conferred not with flesh and blood:

17 neither went I up to Jerusalem to them that were apostles before me: but I went away into Arabia; and again I returned unto Damascus.

After a renewed and fulsome testimony to having been called of God (verses 15, 16), the apostle tells of his "manner of life" after he had become heir to the divine revelation. This demonstrates the complete independence of his apostleship and constitutes an unimpeachable refutation of his opponents, who were obviously trying to discredit him as a sort of "second-hand" apostle.

15 The *good pleasure* gives expression to the sovereign freedom as well as the infinite riches of the divine disposition which is represented at this point, not as preceding, but as coinciding, with the culmination: *to reveal*. The emphasis falls on the sovereignty of the divine grace manifested to Paul. At the same time, however, the apostle stresses the fact that God had much earlier — from his

---

[1] The original δέ is here translated adversatively, as representing a contrast to Paul's own activity; it can also, however, be interpreted conjunctively, inasmuch as in the sequel the preceding is simply continued.

[2] In many important manuscripts, the ὁ Θεός is missing.

mother's womb, as a matter of fact — appointed[3] him for apostleship. Whatever impediments, therefore, he had himself interposed, these could not nullify God's plan for him. For the rest, the certainty of a special separation of his life from birth onward need not rest on a special revelation. What the apostle is talking about here is the counsel of God which governs all things, most especially his work of redemption and the preparation and training of His agents. Jeremiah 1:5 tells us of this, and the fact that Paul is obviously alluding to it shows how greatly he was convinced by God of his special election and appointment. The calling of which he speaks afterward is not identical with this separation,[4] but refers to the event at Damascus. The grace of God, through which this calling took place, was not only its motive but also its means.[5] This grace it was that operated in Paul's calling and made him willing and fit to carry it out.

16, 17 The first effect of God's calling was that He revealed His Son in Paul. Paul's knowledge of Christ as the Son of God rested on God's immediate intervention. The film was, so to speak, removed from his eyes. Then he understood that the Jesus, whom he persecuted and whose name he had up to this point hated and despised, was the Son of God. These verses ascribe the revelation to God, although it had been the Son of God Himself who spoke to him en route to Damascus. This circumstance does not, of course, gainsay the fact that this revelation found its basis in God's good pleasure not only, but can also be named a revelation of the Son by the Father.

More difficult is the exposition of the *in me*. It does not mean to say that the revelation consisted solely of an inter-

---

[3] ἀφορίζω: to separate in the sense of: to set aside for special purpose. The emphasis here falls on this last sense.

[4] Hence there is no basis here for the meaning put forth by some of the old Reformed theologians (Voetius, among others) that Paul was regenerated from childhood onward.

[5] διὰ τῆς χάριτος.

nal experience. According to all the data, it also had an external-objective side. The problem, however, is whether the *in me* stresses especially the internal knowledge and change, consequent upon the revelation in Paul, or whether it could be translated simply as *to me* or, again, be regarded as supplanting the single dative. In support of the first interpretation, scholars point to Rom. 8:23, Gal. 2:20, Col. 1:19, and Rom. 1:18. For the second, they refer to verse 24, and to 1 Tim. 1:16. And, for the third view, they cite Rom. 1:19, 1 Cor. 14:11, and 2 Cor. 4:3. As we see it, too much emphasis ought not to be placed on the internal character of the revelation, and *to me,* or simply *me,* is preferable to *in me* as a translation.[6]

The apostle goes on to say, in the final sentence, to what end this revelation took place. In other words, he is busy here, telling the story, not of his conversion, but of his calling. His special appointment was to preach the gospel to the Gentiles[7] (*cf.* Acts 26:17, 18 and Gal. 2:8). In carrying out this commission, he immediately[8] adopted the policy not to turn to[9] men[10] for counsel; so he could remain

---

[6] The usage occurs more frequently in verbs of knowing, and making known; the ἐν then designates not only the person through whom the communication comes, but also the one who receives it (*cf. Bl.-Debr.,* par. 220, I; *Preuschen-Bauer,* Sp. 406, IV, 4a; *Oepke,* TWNT, III, p. 535, among other places).

[7] τοῖς ἔθνεσιν: here presumably used in the qualified sense of: *heathen.*

[8] εὐθέως οὐ is stronger than οὐκ εὐθέως. It means to say that Paul at once, right from the beginning, was aware of his independence, and that he acted accordingly. This is to say more than that he did not immediately turn to others.

[9] προσανατίθεσθαι τινί: to take counsel with someone, to turn to someone in order to learn his attitude.

[10] Literally *flesh and blood* (*cf.* Eph. 6:12 and Matt. 16:17). It means the human, the creaturely, in itself, in its frailty (*cf.* Acts 2:17 — where, however, *flesh* stands alone); it corresponds to the rabbinical *basjar wedam.*

independent of them. As a matter of fact he even[11] chose not to go[12] to Jerusalem where those were *who were apostles before* (*him*). In one sense this last utterance of his fully acknowledges the calling and authority of the apostles at Jerusalem; in another sense, Paul immediately puts himself on one and the same level with them, even though they were called earlier. However, by now withdrawing into Arabia,[13] a thinly inhabited terrain, extending from the Euphrates in the west far to the north,[14] he immediately turned away from all human influence in order to reflect in solitude on the matter of his calling, and on the turn which his life was now taking.[15]

How long Paul stayed there is something that cannot be made out from this context with certainty. If we are right in concluding that it was not the preaching of the gospel but personal motives, rather, that prompted him to go there, we can more readily conclude that his stay there was comparatively short, and that it took place between his conversion and his preaching at Damascus (of which we read in Acts 9:19, 20). To Damascus, at any rate, he returned, also according to the indications of our text.[16] The name Damascus is here first named in connection with

---

[11] The force of the οὐδέ is not that the apostles could not be reckoned as flesh and blood; it speaks of them rather as the ones who would seem first of all to come to mind.

[12] ἀνῆλθον (in other manuscripts: ἀπ-). ἀνά is, especially in the compound ἀναβαίνω, the regular form for going to Jerusalem.

[13] ἀπῆλθον.

[14] This *Arabia* is not to be thought of as the peninsula stretching far into the south; were that so, one would have to ask whether Paul may have gone to Sinai (*cf.* 4:25). See for the explanation given in the text above Wright-Filson, *The Westminster Historical Atlas to the Bible*, 1945, p. 87.

[15] This interpretation in connection with the contrast (*I conferred not with flesh and blood*) seems more acceptable than the one which has it that we are to think of a tour of gospel preaching.

[16] πάλιν is then construed as having a more or less pleonastic sense, but this can easily be the case in the non-literary linguistic usage (*cf.* Acts 18:21: *Bl.-Debr.*, par. 484).

that return. Paul writes about this period of his life as he would about a matter whose background (the event on the way to Damascus) his readers already knew about in broad outline. Anyhow, the main concern is not fulsomeness of biographical detail, but the evidence that in his apostleship he took an independent position. After his stay in Arabia, too, he did not go to Jerusalem forthwith but remained a while at Damascus. This becomes apparent not only from Acts 9:20 ff. but also from the next following verse of this letter.

ONLY LATER, AND BUT FOR A SHORT TIME, DID PAUL MEET CERTAIN OF THE APOSTLES AT JERUSALEM

1:18-20

18 Then after three years I went up to Jerusalem to visit Cephas, and tarried with him fifteen days.

19 But other of the apostles saw I none, save James the Lord's brother.

20 Now touching the things which I write unto you, behold, before God, I lie not.

18 The following verses also serve to confirm Paul's apostolic independence. Eventually he went to Jerusalem, but only after three years (reckoned from the date of his conversion and calling). In ancient times part of a unit of time (*de termini a quo et ad quem*) was sometimes reckoned a full unit. We cannot say precisely, therefore, how long Paul remained in Damascus (inclusive of his Arabian journey). We can deduce from Acts 9:23 (*cf.* 2 Cor. 11:32-33) that his leaving Damascus took place partly under duress. Otherwise he might have remained at Damascus longer, without visiting Jerusalem. In any event, it took quite a while before he established contact with Peter, and when he did go his purpose was not to secure his authorization as an apostle, or to get instructions from Peter. Such becomes apparent, too, from the word *to visit*,[1] a word which, since it is used in connection with a person, might also have been translated *to make the acquaintance of,* and, at any rate, serves to designate a first meeting. The visit was of a temporary and informative nature. The period is designated plainly as fifteen days. That Paul should have gone to Jerusalem especially to see

---

[1] ἱστορῆσαι (compare ἴστωρ and οἶδα).

Peter, and that he spent his time[2] there with Peter, was probably owing to the latter's peculiar position in the first Christian church. From the whole narrative, with its meticulous citation of time, persons, and the like, it is evident that Paul was and remained fully conscious of his own independence in the preaching of the gospel.

19 The next following communication, namely, that Paul saw none of the other apostles (besides Peter) except James, the brother of the Lord, has the same bearing. James was not one of the twelve. Moreover, the expression used in the Greek does not necessarily imply that Paul is here reckoning him as one of the apostles;[3] it would, in fact, tend to point the other way.[4] Still, on the basis of general considerations, one could accept the view that Paul

---

[2] πρός with the accusative, unlike παρά plus the dative, suggests an *active* association (*cf.* John 1:1).

[3] In other words, we need not regard the εἰ μή as designating an exception (to ἕτερον τῶν ἀποστόλων); it can also be taken as the equivalent of ἀλλά, a contrasting complement in the sense of: *except that I did see* (*cf.* Mt. 12:4, Mark 13:32, and see *Bl.-Debr.*, par. 448). The mention of James in this connection would then be motivated by his important position (see text of Exposition).

[4] After all, what we really have in the text is this: "other (than Peter) of the apostles I saw none." If we accept the view that Paul is also including James among the apostles in his last clause, we are really saying that Paul in that clause is retracting what he said in his first clause (so, *e.g.*, Zahn, Greijdanus, and others). Still, as we see it, it remains questionable whether we can justifiably take the syntax with this kind of logical severity. For this would mean that besides Peter and James Paul had met nobody in Jerusalem — a conclusion which, on the basis of other considerations, is less acceptable. Moreover, the second clause can be regarded as an exception to what has been predicated in the first, without sacrificing the meaning of the first. After all, there were many apostles besides Peter (and James): compare verse 17. That Paul did not immediately think of James may be owing to the fact that a kind of difference still obtained between Peter and the other apostles, on the one hand, and James, on the other. The argument based on the syntax seems to us, therefore, too subtle to determine the matter.

was here counting him among the apostles.[5] A particular appearance of the Risen One had fallen to his share (1 Cor. 15:7; *cf.* 1 Cor. 14:1-5). In part, surely, on the basis of that fact, he had a special place in the church at Jerusalem. The addendum, *the Lord's brother,* distinguishes him from other persons of that name, among whom there were or had been apostles (namely, James, the son of Zebedee; and James, the son of Alphaeus). But James is an honorable name. We read of this James' special position in Acts 12:17, 15:13, 21:18, and in Gal. 2:9, 12.

20 In this verse Paul confirms everything he has said with an oath. After all, nothing less is at stake than the validity and independence of his apostleship. And he defends these against the attacks made against him by an appeal to the highest Judge.

---

[5] There is no fixed and regular mode of designation. In the Acts (14:4 and 14) Paul and Barnabas are also named apostles, just as Paul himself repeatedly calls himself an apostle. In 1 Cor. 15:5, 7 the apostles and the twelve are clearly distinguished from each other. A looser mode of designation occurs also in such places as Rom. 16:7, 2 Cor. 11:5, 13, and 1 Thess. 2:7. The problem is whether one can adopt the principle that by the ἀπόστολοι in this broader sense only those persons are intended who were personally called to the preaching of the gospel by the Risen One (*cf.* Rengstorf, *TWNT,* I, p. 423, under ἀπόστολος). Others think that itinerant Christian preachers of various kinds also were called apostles, or, at least, laid claim to the title (*cf.* 2 Cor. 11:5-13, 12:11: see, *e.g.,* Oepke, *op. cit.,* p. 27). The inference then is that there was a broader and a narrower sense in which the term *apostles* was used. No satisfactory solution to the problem has yet been given (for the various opinions, see, *e.g.,* Holger Mosbeck, *Apostolos in the New Testament, Studia Theologica,* Lund, 1947, pp. 166-200). In any event it is not strange at all that James, the brother of the Lord, to whom Jesus appeared after His resurrection, should here be reckoned alongside of Peter among the apostles.

TO THE CHURCHES IN JUDAEA ALSO PAUL WAS PERSONALLY UNKNOWN

1:21-24

21 Then I came into the regions of Syria and Cilicia.

22 And I was still unknown by face unto the churches of Judaea which were in Christ:

23 but they only heard say, He that once persecuted us now preacheth the faith of which he once made havoc;

24 and they glorified God in me.

21 Also this conclusion of Chapter 1, beginning as it does with verse 1, serves to point up the independence of Paul's apostleship over against the other apostles. After the visit to Jerusalem narrated in verse 18, Paul went into distant lands as a preacher of the gospel, outside the direct sphere of influence of the apostles. The expression, *the regions of Syria and Cilicia,* is very general. Presumably we are not to take this *Syria* as referring to the whole Roman province of that name (to which Palestine also belonged: *cf.* Luke 2:2, and other places), but rather as designating Antioch and its environs, where Paul preached the gospel (*cf.* Acts 11:25). Of his stay in Cilicia,[1] the Acts also give an account (9:30). He tarried there a while, that is, in Tarsus; this was before Barnabas invited him to Antioch. Because, however, Paul speaks first in

---

[1] Despite some variant textual evidence, we shall have to read the Κιλικίας as accompanied by the article. In that way Cilicia takes on an independence of its own alongside of Syria, with which it constituted a kind of political unit. Actually, Cilicia was an independent province, but one which, owing to its modest size, was not granted an independent government by the first caesars, and therefore came under the jurisdiction of the governor of Syria (*cf.* J. Weiss, HRE, X, 3rd edit., 1901, p. 561). This more modest significance of Cilicia may account for its being named second in the text.

this connection of Syria, and then of Cilicia, we may suppose that he is not concerned to give a chronologically arranged narrative of his experiences in the fourteen years preceding his trip to Jerusalem (referred to in 2:1), but only to give a general idea of the places in which he was occupied during that time. So construed, and viewed from the vantage point of Jerusalem, the geographical order, Syria-Cilicia, was a natural one. Nor does Paul speak of the circumstances under which he left Jerusalem, and of his first missionary journey, which must have taken place during his stay in Syria, and within these fourteen years (see the Exposition for 2:1 below). But such considerations are not relevant here. The issue at present is his relationship with the other apostles, and the great distance that separated him from them for years.

22 Paul had moved so little within the sphere of influence of the apostles that the churches in Judaea did not know[2] him personally.[3] This unfamiliarity in no way conflicts with what is reported in Acts 8:3 and 9:1 concerning the scope of Paul's persecution of the Christians — a scope which extended beyond the pale of Jerusalem. For, even though here and there a person in the church may have known him, Paul certainly as a persecutor never put in his appearance in the assemblies of the churches of Judaea. Moreover, he is speaking at the moment of a much later state of affairs, and of the fact that as a preacher of the gospel he had never presented himself to these Judaean churches.

The words, *which were in Christ,* in general indicate the Christian character of these churches, in distinction from the Jewish communions. The expression *in Christ,* which Paul uses in all kinds of connections, and appears now for the first time in this letter, must be taken corpora-

---

[2] ἤμην ἀγνούμενος: periphrastic, designating a continuous condition.

[3] τῷ προσώπῳ: dative of relation: by face, *in person.*

tively: it states that the church is included in the redemptive work of Christ[4] and is subjectively governed and moved by Him.

Of importance, further, is what is to be understood by *Judaea* as it is here used. The agreement between this passage and that of Acts 9:28-29 depends to a considerable extent upon how this Judaea is interpreted. If Jerusalem is included in it, the agreement is hard to come by. The problem, however, is whether we can, within the pale of our text, rule Jerusalem out, and not become arbitrary in doing so. It is generally denied that this can be done. But we can also ask the question whether we are not contradicting Paul himself when, in view of what is told us in verses 28 and 29, we propose to include Jerusalem within the pale of Judaea. We certainly read nothing about Paul keeping himself in hiding during his visit to Peter or travelling *incognito* into Jerusalem. Nor is there the least occasion to suppose that he did so. He met only a few of the *apostles*. But the most natural assumption would be that he also had contact with the church at Jerusalem. Hence, in view of the fact that in verse 18 we read only about Jerusalem, we can without arbitrariness and with all plausibility construe the Judaea of verse 22 as referring to

---

[4] The preposition ἐν would seem according to the original sense to imply designation of place, but is not here intended in a spatial-mystical sense, as though Christ were being represented as the spiritual element or medium in which the believers move (as is held by A. Deissmann, *Paulus*, 2, 1952, p. 106 ff.). It is intended in the corporative sense. Christ is the second Adam, in whom the believers are incorporated in the sense that they belong to the new order of life and of grace as distinguished from the order represented by the first Adam (*cf.* Oepke, TWNT, II, pp. 536-538 under ἐν). The unintermittent use of this phrase gives it a stereotyped character, and it is, of course, a question in how far the original force of place-designation is to be observed in it. As a matter of fact this *in Christ* represents, in a remarkable and comprehensive way, the whole profound view Paul unfolds in his letters concerning the significance for the believers of the salvation that has appeared in Christ.

the Jewish country, and leave Jerusalem out of considera-tion here.[5] In other words what Paul wants to say in verse 22 is that, after his brief stay in Jerusalem, he had not lingered in the vicinity, but immediately taken off for remote areas.

23 This verse adds to the foregoing the thought that the churches in Jewish Judaea had learned of Paul's con-version and preaching only by hearsay.[6] There is no point in making a problem out of who the speakers are that are represented here as talking in direct discourse.[7] Such things as these — the idea is — the people were saying among each other. Probably there were some among them who had been the personal victims of Paul's perse-cuting zeal; these would then have been outside of the city either because they fled there (*cf.* Acts 8:1-3), or because they were there when Paul molested them (*cf.* Acts 9:1-2).

By *faith* which is used here as the object of the preach-ing (*he preacheth the faith*) the *content* of faith is pre-sumably intended (*fides quae creditur*). On the other hand, the subjective meaning of the faith, (*fides qua credi-*

---

[5] Compare Mt. 3:5, 4:25, John 3:22, Acts 1:8, 8:1, and 26:20. A further problem is whether the Ἰουδαία used here refers solely to Judaea or also to the entire Jewish country, inclusive, *e.g.*, of Samaria and Galilee. The name is not always used in the same sense, and sometimes denominates the original territory of Judaea, sometimes the Roman province in the time of Pilate (Judaea and Idumea), and then again the whole of Palestine, such as, *e.g.*, was governed by Herod the Great and Agrippa I (*cf.*, *e.g.*, De Witt Burton, *Galatians* (ICC), pp. 435-436). Presumably the designation in this context ought not to be taken in a too restricted sense, in view of the spread of the Christian faith in the time of which Paul is writing (*cf.* Acts 9:31), and the nature of the subject matter with which he is dealing. Not only in the immediate vicinity of Jerusa-lem, but also farther to the north, gospel work was going on out of the Jerusalem base, and there too contact with the apostles had been established. Moreover, Paul is taking pains to make the point that all these years he has been standing outside of this activity.

[6] The periphrastic again, as in Note 2 given above.

[7] The ὅτι is to be taken as direct discourse.

tur), would serve better as the object of the persecution[8] (*of which he once made havoc*). Apparently the exclusive-objective significance of the faith (*cf., e.g.,* Jude 20) is not what we have here, but, rather, a transition towards it.

24 The final thought, namely, that these churches glorified God in Paul, incidentally suggests that these churches did *not* doubt the genuineness and integrity of Paul's calling and preaching. And that, if you please, from those who had suffered so much on his account! How different the attitude in the churches of Galatia, even though these had experienced only good from him, and had not the slightest reason to doubt his apostolic calling and authority!

---

[8] ἐπόρθει: compare the Exposition of verse 13.

CHAPTER II

ACKNOWLEDGMENT OF PAUL'S MISSIONARY COMMISSION BY THE APOSTOLIC CONFERENCE

2:1-10

1 Then after the space of fourteen years I went up again to Jerusalem with Barnabas, taking Titus also with me.

2 And I went up by revelation; and I laid before them the gospel which I preach among the Gentiles but privately before them who were of repute, lest by any means I should be running, or had run, in vain.

3 But not even Titus who was with me, being a Greek, was compelled to be circumcised:

4 and that because of the false brethren privily brought in, who came in privily to spy out our liberty which we have in Christ Jesus, that they might bring us into bondage:

5 to whom we gave place in the way of subjection, no, not for an hour; that the truth of the gospel might continue with you.

6 But from those who were reputed to be somewhat (whatsoever they were, it maketh no matter to me: God accepteth not man's person) — they, I say, who were of repute imparted nothing to me:

7 but contrariwise, when they saw that I had been entrusted with the gospel of the uncircumcision, even as Peter with *the gospel* of the circumcision

8 (for he that wrought for Peter unto the apostleship of the circumcision wrought for me also unto the Gentiles);

9 and when they perceived the grace that was given unto me, James and Cephas and John, they who were reputed to be pillars, gave to me and Barnabas the right hands of fellowship, that we should go unto the Gentiles, and they unto the circumcision;

10 only *they would* that we should remember the poor; which very thing I was also zealous to do.

This section continues the defense of Paul's apostolic qualifications. The argument now, however, no longer concerns solely his independence in relation to the apostles at Jerusalem, but concerns also their acquiescence with him. This acquiescence was demonstrated when the issue of missions to the Gentiles was discussed at the so-called apostolic council at Jerusalem.

1 Once more (*cf.* 1:18, 21) the sentence begins with *then*,[1] and once more a segment of time is indicated which sheds light on the relationship existing between Paul and the apostles at Jerusalem. Now the time-period indicated comprises no fewer than fourteen years,[2] fourteen years, of course, in which the *termini a quo* and *ad quem* perhaps are being reckoned as a full year. It is self-evident that the *terminus a quo* is not again (as in 1:18) to be reckoned from the date of Paul's conversion, but from the visit to Jerusalem mentioned in verse 21. Throughout this time, nothing had happened that spelled any change in his relations with the other apostles or was particularly deserving of mention. This period was long enough certainly, if it be assumed as necessary, for Paul to become fully conscious of his own calling, and to develop himself in his independence.

The reason why Paul mentions this visit of fourteen years later is not quite the same as that of the visit designated in 1:18 ff. At issue *there* was the formal consideration of his authority as apostle; at issue *here* in 2:1 is material agreement about a very pressing point: whether the

---

[1] ἔπειτα

[2] διά plus the genitive is here used to designate the ending of a period of time. More than μετά with the accusative, it puts the emphasis on the length of the elapsed time (*cf.* Mark 2:1 and Acts 24:17).

Gentiles are bound by the law of Moses. The use of *again*[3] need not mean: for the second time. It does not rule out the possibility of a visit sometime between the occasions indicated in 1:18 and 2:1 (see below). Barnabas and Titus are now named as companions on the journey. Barnabas was the man who had immediately taken Paul's part (*cf.* Acts 9:27), was intimately involved in all sorts of work with Paul (Acts 11:25, 30; 12:25; 13:2 ff.) and at the same time, since way back, had had certain relations with the leaders and the church at Jerusalem (*cf.* Acts 4:36, 37; 9:27; and 10:22), and he was, probably because of his having originally come from Cyprus (Acts 4:37), peculiarly fitted to serve in a mediating capacity in the situation narrated here. Presumably the companionship of this journey antedated the estrangement between Paul and Barnabas reported in Acts 15:39.

The way in which Titus is brought into the account,[4] suggests that he had a more subordinate position and that his going along was based on Paul's initiative. He was a Gentile, and was not circumcised. His presence with Paul, consequently, amounted to a living, personal example of Paul's position, and served very well to drive Paul's conviction home to others. In the correspondence between Paul and the church at Corinth, Titus played an important role (2 Cor. 2:13, 7:6, and other places; *cf.,* however, also 2 Tim. 4:10 and Titus 1:4).

---

[3] πάλιν: this word is missing in some manuscripts. Perhaps it was omitted because it was interpreted as meaning *for the second time,* whereas the journey in question was regarded by the scribe as not the first journey of the apostle after that mentioned in 1:18. πάλιν can, however, also mean *anew* in the general sense, without indication of the number of times involved (*cf.* John 18:27). So interpreted it might easily have been introduced in connection with 1:18. A decision in the matter is difficult to give, and is comparatively unimportant, if only we keep the real meaning of the word in mind.

[4] συνπαραλαβών.

The problem which has given occasion for much discussion and difference of opinion is *which journey of Paul to Jerusalem is here being referred to*; and, more specifically, whether it can be identified with one of Paul's journeys to Jerusalem as reported in the Acts. The journey mentioned in Acts 18:22 cannot be involved here (for a contrary judgment, see E. Barnikol, *Die drei Jerusalemreisen des Paulus,* 1929). No arguments can be found to support the view, either in the letter to the Galatians, or in the Acts. More formidable is the case for the view, taken by various scholars, that the journey of Gal. 2:1 is identical with the collection-journey of Acts 11:30 (cf. 12:25). Proponents of this view are especially impressed by the consideration that Paul could not fail to mention this trip in this connection without doing violence to the truth, and they point particularly to his oath in 1:20. However, as we see it, this sort of argumentation proceeds from a mistaken assumption, namely, that the apostle was engaged here in giving a comprehensive survey of the relations he had had, during his apostleship, with Jerusalem and the leaders of the church at that place. This is something which the apostle at no point claims to be doing. His purpose is simply, on the one hand, to set forth his independence as an apostle over against his challengers, and, on the other, his agreement with the apostles. In 1:16 ff. that first issue is up for consideration: he had not received his calling from men, but from Christ, and he had not carried it out as bound to the reins of the other apostles, but had learned how to do it in his own right. Now, in Chapter 2, the issue is the material question between him and his opponents in Galatia and the attitude of the apostles towards this question (see Exposition above). Hence the possibility of yet another journey intervening between those of Chapters 1 and 2 need not be ruled out by such argumentation, nor denominated a suppression of the full truth. All one can infer from the facts in the matter is that such another journey was of no importance for what Paul wants to accomplish in this letter.

Once one has rid himself of the idea that Paul wants to give a summary here of all his trips to Jerusalem, one is much more open to the view that identifies the journey of 2:1 with the one to the so-called apostolic council (Acts 15) rather than with the "collection-journey" of Acts 11:30. In both accounts, after all, despite all the differences in the mode of description, the purpose of the journey is stated to be the settlement of the differences concerning Gentile Christians. The differences between Paul's account in Galatians 2 and that of Acts 15 can be discussed in what follows below: now it may suffice to say that these differences are not materially contradictory, and take their rise in the difference of point of view. In our letter the conference at Jerusalem is described in a polemical-apologetical argument; in Acts 15 it is described in a more impersonal and generally historical narrative (see the Exposition).

Another matter is this: it is said that on the basis of internal evidence, that is, on the basis of grounds given in the letter itself, the identification of the visit of Acts 15 and Galatians 2 must be challenged. The most important of these alleged internal grounds are probably these: (a) that the attitude of Peter (described in Gal. 2:11-14) at Antioch is not to be accounted for if the decision reported in Acts 15 had been taken only a short time before; and (b) that it is incredible to suppose that, if Paul in this letter to the Galatians could have had the support of the apostolic council, he would have done anything but make a simple appeal to the decisions of Jerusalem in his opposition to the Judaistic contenders. For a further account of these arguments, see the Introduction, V.

So far as the first of these arguments goes, there is no denying a certain disparity between Peter's attitude at Antioch and the decisions taken at Jerusalem as described in Acts 15. This disparity exists, however, also within the pale of Galatians 2. Paul even speaks in 2:13 of a certain "dissembling." However, what is called inexplicable in Peter's attitude is something for which Peter is accountable, and cannot be removed by making the event of Galatians 2 a different event from that of Acts 15. In fairness, however, it should also be kept in mind that in the formal sense, too, there was a certain difference between the decisions approved at Jerusalem (according to Acts 15) and what Peter felt that he had to disapprove of at Antioch (according to Galatians 2). The issue at Jerusalem, also according to Acts 15, was the freedom of the Gentiles, and the issue at Antioch was the binding of the Jews to the ceremonial law. Because Peter did not draw the right conclusions from what had been decided at Jerusalem and because Paul had to reprimand him for his error, we can hardly speak of a flagrant disparity in Peter's attitude. On this ground, then, the identity of the visits of Acts 15 and Galatians 2:1 ff. cannot be successfully challenged.

In order to judge of the worth of the second argument indicated above, one would have to be very familiar with the situation in the churches of Galatia, and be able to prove that the Judaistic contenders would have allowed themselves to be silenced by an appeal to what the apostles had endorsed. It is true, they apparently wanted to undermine Paul's authority by presenting him as the least authentic among the apostles. But that they themselves were not loyally subject to those other apostles is clear enough from the fact that they wanted to force the Gentiles to be circumcised. The absence of any appeal, consequently, to the decisions of Acts 15 in Galatians does not constitute a ground for holding that those decisions had not been taken when Paul wrote this letter. Moreover, it is quite in accord with the whole bearing of this letter that Paul did not want to borrow his authority in the matter of circumcision from the apostles, nor from an appeal to what they approved of as settling the matter. He wanted to determine this issue on objective-religious and Christological grounds, and so to safeguard the churches against the domination of Judaism.

As we see it, consequently, there is nothing in the evidence adduced that would make for a justifiable identification of the journey of Galatians 2 with that of Acts 11 and 12 rather than with that of Acts 15. On the contrary, it is necessary to point out the weighty objections to such a view. Nothing in Acts 11 and 12 suggests that the issue of the Gentiles as defined in Galatians 2 was discussed during the "collection-journey." For all these reasons, we think it most justified, in explaining Galatians 2, to regard the identity of the council in Jerusalem of Acts 15 with that of Galatians 2 our proper point of departure. Naturally, this does not mean that various points of difference will not on occasion have to be discussed.

2 Paul's declaration that he went to Jerusalem on the basis of, and in agreement with, a revelation,[5] tells us that he took this important step neither arbitrarily nor by way of experiment, but in the strength of divine commissioning and empowerment. Nor is it in conflict with this view that he also went on assignment from the church at Antioch (Acts 15:1). It is even possible that the revelation did not come to him personally (*cf.* Acts 13:2, 4). But the conclusion lies ready at hand that he received this revelation when he was in a state of doubt concerning which direction the way of the Lord pointed, and that he received certainty about the desirability of the journey to Jerusalem. In the next following words we first learn of the real purpose of the journey, although this purpose is expressed in a paratactical construction. Hence when we read further *and I laid before*[6] *them the gospel* this does not mean to

---

[5] κατὰ ἀποκάλυψιν.
[6] Ἀνατίθεμαι: *to submit for judgment.*

say that Paul had begun to feel insecure about the content of his gospel. But it was necessary that everybody should not be going his own way. This was a communal matter. And especially the mother-church at Jerusalem and its most prominent leaders ought to share in this decision. These leaders are designated as those *who were of repute*.[7] This need not be interpreted as an ironical remark; it positively is not that. True, it is remarkable that the expression occurs four times. Such repetition may imply that Paul is here taking over a phrase used by the opponents in designating the most prominent leaders at Jerusalem.[8] The persons involved are, according to verse 9, apparently in the first place Peter, John, and James. To these he presented his matter *privately*. In other words, there were public and private discussions. The purpose of these private discussions was to circumvent[9] the possibility that, by yielding to the wishes of the Judaizers, Paul's work, at least that of the past, should practically be made useless. This does not mean to say that Paul would have stood ready *a priori* to abide by the decision of the leaders at Jerusalem — for that would have been to declare his apostleship and his missionary commission dependent upon

---

[7] οἱ δοκοῦντες, used in the absolute sense here, and differing therefore from verse 6a and 9.

[8] Compare Kittel, TWNT, II, p. 236, under δοκέω.

[9] *Lest by any means I should . . . ..* The meaning of μή πως, meanwhile is not very clear. Instead of the indicative ἔδραμον, one would expect a subjunctive. This indicative makes it uncertain, too, how τρέχω should be construed, whether as an indicative or subjunctive. Some, consequently, want to interpret the μή πως not as a final predication, but as introduction to an indirect question, the answer to which is to be negative: I laid the Gospel before them (together with the question) whether in their judgment I had been running in vain (*cf.* for this use, 1 Thess. 3:5). Such an interpretation would also give a clearer expression to Paul's independence as compared with the others. On such a basis, one must presumably ascribe the use of the indicative to the less discriminating practice of the Koine. The bearing of the final clause, then, must be viewed from the vantage point of those to whom Paul put the question.

their views. However, if at Jerusalem it was proposed to do as the Judaizers wished, those who proposed it had better know that this would be tantamount to obliterating the work which Paul had done with so much exertion.[10] If the Gentiles also had to subject themselves to the law of Moses, Paul might as well begin all over again from the very start.

3 Anticipating the favorable issue of the discussions, Paul writes: but *not even Titus* (an uncircumcised Christian from among the Gentiles[11]) was compelled to be circumcised. His presence with Paul raised the whole problem in palpably concrete form, and yet, as it turned out, was not the occasion for laying down circumcision as a *sine qua non*. That then practically settled the matter. Certainly if Titus, as a member of the delegation,[12] could move about among Jewish Christians, one could hardly lay down a more exacting requirement for the conduct of Gentiles among each other.

This is the first point at which circumcision is mentioned in the letter. That it is, however, the great point of contention in the whole controversy between Paul and his opponents is the tacit assumption of the entire book of Galatians.

4 It is difficult to make out the precise significance of verse 4. It may be that what we have in this verse, al-

---

[10] τρέχω: to run hard as in a race (*cf.* Phil. 2:16).

[11] Ἕλλην need not imply that he was a Greek by nationality, but only that he came from a non-Jewish, pagan sphere of life which, in those days, found in the Greek language its general means of communication (*cf.* Mark 7:26).

[12] For this reason, and not first of all because of his Gentile descent, the ἀλλ' οὐδέ, *but not even,* is used. Certainly not the fact that he was a Greek could have obligated him more than others to be circumcised, but the fact that, together with Paul (ὁ σὺν ἐμοί), he had to go to Jewish Christians.

though it does not quite fit the syntax,[13] is a hint as to the source from which the opposition at Jerusalem came, and by whom the demand that Titus be circumcised was

---

[13] Presumably verse 4 is to be taken together with verse 3, and to be regarded as an appositive amplifier in which it is said that although Titus was not compelled to submit to circumcision by the leading figures at Jerusalem, there nevertheless were persons in Jerusalem who demanded it. That is Explanation One. There is another view, which, for purposes of reference, can be called Explanation Two. If we prefer not to connect verse 4 with verse 3, that is, to regard verse 3 as a new predication, we must interpret it as an anacoluthon. We must then surmise that, hard upon the beginning of verse 4, a verb should be understood, such as: *there was conflict* or *I had to be on my guard*, presumably in logical connection with verse 2, but that owing to the relative οἷς, the sentence took another turn and was not completed. All this, of course, holds only if the rendering οἷς οὐδέ of verse 5 is original. Most manuscripts have it. In one, however, the words are omitted. The translation, then, would be: because of the false brethren . . . we gave ground for a moment (in going to Jerusalem, that is; so, e.g., Th. Zahn, *Der Brief des Paulus an die Galater*, 1922, p. 89 ff.). In some manuscripts, too, only the οἷς is missing. That makes for the translation: but for the sake of the false brethren we did not give ground for a moment. Finally there are some indications which point to a rendering without the οὐδέ. That gives the result: but because of the false brethren (we (or, Titus?) had to give way), for the sake of whom we yielded for a time. All of these later readings have weak textual support. Apparently a certain confusion arose because of the difficult syntactical construction offered by the text we are following. So regarded, the omission of οἷς can easily be explained: it makes for no essential change in the sentence. It is more difficult to explain the absence of οὐδέ, however, for the absence of this word reverses the sense of the passage. In its absence, it is difficult to come to any conclusion other than that Titus did submit to circumcision (Zahn's interpretation seems forced). And that would be in conflict with the whole bearing of the contention. Irrespective, therefore, of how this interpretation arose, it is by virtue both of the weak textual support and of its unreasonableness, unacceptable to us.

Finally the question still remains whether the δέ of verse 4 is original. Marcion omitted it, apparently to avoid an about-face over against verse 3. It can, however, also be taken with transitional force. See the translation, and see Explanation One. To regard it as an adversative is to construe verse 4 as an anacoluthon. See Explanation Two. The δέ is textually firmly verified.

proposed. In designating those persons *the false brethren,* Paul challenges their right to belong to the church. They made their approach as brothers in the Lord, and apparently were received as such also, and so were granted the right to speak in the church. But the way in which they entered (a stealthy, dishonest way,[14] concealing their real motives), and their conduct after they were in, marked them as false and unauthentic members of the church. Paul calls the real purpose for which they stole in: *to spy out our liberty which we have in Christ Jesus.* The figure is that of a spy who infiltrates the enemy camp, plays the part of a friend to the cause, and so gets to learn the strategic situation of the opponent. By *our liberty* the apostle means, as becomes more evidently apparent in the following chapter, the freedom from the law brought by Christ. This freedom concerns not only the curse of the law, and the ethical impotence in which sinful man confronts the demand of the law — an impotence which Christ removes — but also the content of the law in its historical, Mosaic form. If, on the one hand, it is plain also from the Galatians, that the apostle continues to maintain the fulfillment of the law as the purpose of the Christian life (*cf.* 5:14, 23; Rom. 8:4; 13:8, and other places); on the other, his insistence is plain also that the real content of the law can be known only in consideration of the finished work of Christ. What stands between the law and the believers, in respect not merely of the results of transgressing the law and the possibility of fulfilling it, but in respect also of establishing the content of the law, is: Christ. It is in that comprehensive sense that the believers in Christ Jesus can be said to be free (of the law). And it was this inalien-

---

[14] παρείσακτος: only here in the New Testament is the meaning: *stole into.*

able possession[15] of the church which the false brethren tried to take away from it, by trying to bring it once more under the dominion of the law. The thing the apostle is here describing was in general the effort of the Judaistic zealots in the church, but it was particularly the effort of those whom Paul had come to know as his opponents in Jerusalem.

5 According to the translation which we are following,[16] the apostle describes his attitude and that of his fellows as adamant. At issue, after all, was not merely the question of whether or not Titus ought to be circumcised, but also that of *the truth of the gospel*: that is, its true, unmodified content.[17] In other instances Paul wanted to give in, to accommodate himself, in order to aid the influence of the gospel (*cf.* 5:12, 1 Cor. 9:19-23, Acts 16:3, 21:23 ff.). But this time the issue was drawn *in optima forma* and he knew no yielding. And Paul indicates that in taking this resolute stand he had the churches of Galatia in his mind's eye. He wanted no damage done to the essence of the gospel once preached to them.[18]

---

[15] Compare the present: ἔχομεν.

[16] Compare Footnote 13.

[17] ἡ ἀλήθεια τοῦ εὐαγγελίου can be translated formally as "the true gospel" (so, *e.g.*, Oepke); others translate: in order that the gospel might preserve its truth, that is, its validity (so Bultmann, TWNT, I, p. 242). As we see it, the major referent here is the truth as the content of the gospel.

[18] The opponents of the South Galatian hypothesis say that we need not infer from πρὸς ὑμᾶς that Paul had the church of Galatia in mind; ὑμᾶς is then taken in an ideal, not in a personal sense: You Gentiles. Even though the *with you* which is used here cannot be taken as proof positive that the apostle knew the churches of Galatia already when he was still in Jerusalem, and he must therefore have visited them on his first missionary journey (in the *province* of Galatia), still, the explanation of πρὸς ὑμᾶς διαμείνῃ from the South Galatian point of view is the more natural one. πρὸς ὑμᾶς, more than πρὸς ὑμῖν, stresses the generally objective in distinction from the local. Thence the force: that the truth *in its bearing on you* might continue.

6 The rhetorical structure of this verse, too, is hard to analyze.[19] The manner in which the apostle writes betrays a certain excitement. Again he refers to the leaders at Jerusalem as *those who were reputed* (see the Exposition of verse 2), this time with the amplification: *to be somewhat*. Again he is not talking in ironical vein in disparagement of those leaders — as a matter of fact, he is even now in the act of saying that they put no impediments in his way — but, all the same, there lurks in this continuous repetition (*cf.* verse 9), and in the parenthetically appended *whatsoever they are,* and the like, an indirect but undeniable criticism of the way in which others were trying to play off the prestige of these leaders against him. Hence, while Paul on the one hand can now cite the approbation of his career by those leaders, on the other he lets it be felt, with a certain deliberateness, that he was less impressed by the prestige of those leaders than they who are apparently trying to convince him and others of its scope and importance. It was merely the agreement between him and the other apostles that he wanted to stress; accordingly, there was no reason to play himself off against them. By the *whatsoever they were* Paul is certainly suggesting the unusual privilege which the apostles had once enjoyed,[20] namely, their association with Jesus. But that too is irrelevant to his present purpose. Nor does he report his

---

[19] As we see it, this passage is a true anacoluthon. Some have tried to avoid construing it as such by making the τῶν δοκούντων independent (as in verse 2) and by making the εἶναι τι subordinate to οὐδέν μοι διαφέρει. The translation would then read: *but it maketh no matter to me to be somewhat in the estimation of those who were of repute.* But the expression εἶναι τι ἀπό τινος does not thus occur. Nor does the context suggest any wish on Paul's part to separate himself from the leaders at Jerusalem so brusquely as not to care at all about their estimate of him.

[20] Others construe the ἦσαν as referring to the period of time involved in the transactions, and interpret the ποτέ not as a temporal modifier but as a generalizing addendum to the ὁποῖοι as in the Latin *cumque* (in this connection, therefore: *qualescumque*). However, such a construction does not occur in the New Testament.

agreement with them in order to cover himself with their prestige. For: *God accepteth no man's person.*[21] And everything depends upon God's judgment. If the principle at stake were wrong, Paul would not approve it because it has the support of people with reputation. He had not gone to Jerusalem to subject himself to the judgment of the apostles; he went rather to convince them of the rightness of his stand.

The clause interrupted by the parenthesis is not completed,[22] but is begun anew,[23] this time in active form, with *who were of repute* serving as the subject. There has been much difference of opinion about the meaning of the word translated *to impart* in the version above.[24] As we see it, this translation is good; it takes account, too, of the literal meaning: to impose something. True, this use of the original term does not occur elsewhere in the New Testament.[25] But this means little, in view of the fact that the term itself occurs only here and in 1:16. The meaning,

---

[21] The expression is Hebraic. It is used several times in reference to God (*cf.* Deut. 10:17). As used here also the expression has something of an appeal to *what is written* in it. The word that gets the stress is πρόσωπον: God does not judge by the countenance, by externalities. Judging by appearances is something regularly regarded as illegitimate in judgment at law (*cf.* Lev. 19:15). Paul has conducted his affairs in full consciousness cf the fact that God would require an accounting of his deeds.

[22] To judge from its conclusion, we can say that the clause should have ended somewhat as follows: οὐδέν μοι προσανετέθη or οὐδὲν παρελαβόμην.

[23] The γάρ explains nothing here; it seems to be used solely to confirm the unexpressed thought of the anacoluthon.

[24] The general tendency is to translate the word in harmony with 1:16: to submit for consideration, to confer with. Some go on to suggest that Paul had indeed called for a decision, but they, from their side, did not care for advice from him (so Zahn, *op. cit.,* and Behm, *TWNT,* I, pp. 355-356). This explanation does not suit the context at all. See for the translation and exposition used above in the text, *e.g.,* H. Lietzmann, *An die Galater,* 2nd. edit., 1923, p. 12 and Oepke, *op. cit.*

[25] See for the usage elsewhere Oepke, *op. cit.,* pp. 37-38.

then, ought to be clear. The leaders at Jerusalem have laid no more upon Paul in the way of obligation in his missionary work among the Gentiles than he himself had already taken cognizance of. And the specific thrust of this bears on the matter of observing the Jewish ceremonies (*cf.* Acts 15:28).[26]

7-9 Now comes the positive element.[27] The construction is again rather difficult; verse 8 gives rise to another parenthesis, though without disturbing the context of meaning. The words *when they saw* indicate that the leaders acted not only upon Paul's argumentation, but upon their own recognition and conviction of his case. In the construction *the gospel of the (un) circumcision,* the genitive looks to the address[28] of the gospel preaching, not to its content. The gospel was in both instances the same gospel. The fact that the gospel of the circumcision[29] is identified specifically with Peter, and that of the uncircumcision with Paul himself, is certainly owing to the leading role of these two. The parenthesis of verse 8 gives the reason for the dawning insight that the preaching of the gospel had been entrusted to Paul as well as to Peter. The same God empowered both of them, and caused His cooperation in the apostolic ministry of both[30] to become plainly evident. The reference presumably is to the signs and wonders and conversions which were fruits of the labor.

---

[26] There we read of πλέον ἐπιτίθεσθαι βάρος.

[27] This positive element is introduced by ἀλλὰ τουναντίον, which must, in turn, be connected with δεξιὰς ἔδωκαν of verse 9, not with ἰδόντες.

[28] τῆς ἀκροβυστίας, like τῆς περιτομῆς must be taken as an objective genitive.

[29] We are to think presumably of the preaching among still unconverted Jews in and outside of the city of Jerusalem.

[30] ἐνεργήσας . . . ἐνήργησεν: in order to make the same divine influence manifest. In the first instance it is construed with the dative *commodi* (Πέτρῳ), in the second with εἰς. Hence the thought is aimed not so much at the internal essence as at the effect of the divine power.

Apostleship in this connection has reference not to the commission, the mandate (Acts 1:25, Rom. 1:5), but to the carrying out of it, the execution. By constantly making Paul's work among the Gentiles the counterpart[31] of Peter's work among the Jews, the conference at Jerusalem acknowledged Paul in his full right. As for the divine commission and authorization of Peter — that was already a firm conviction for those who met there. Remarkable in this account is the very great importance attached to external manifestation of the divine power in the gospel work. This manifestation constitutes not the condition, it is true, but the seal (1 Cor. 9:2) and the signs (2 Cor. 12:12) of the apostolic genuineness.

Verse 9 continues the thought of verse 7. *The grace* comprises in one word what has been said in verses 7 and 8, that is, the ministry of the gospel and the divine power manifesting itself in this ministry, qualified, both of them, as an undeserved gift. This time, because of the importance of the decision here announced, *they who were reputed* are named by name. James is mentioned first — a circumstance from which his special position at Jerusalem can be deduced (*cf.* Acts 12:17, 15:13, 21:18; *cf.* the Exposition of 1:19). Peter is called Cephas.[32] The Aramaic form suggests the life at Jerusalem. John can refer only to the son of Zebedee. Some, it is true, have wanted to make this name refer to John Mark, in order to support a hypothesis about the early death of John the son of Zebedee. The arbitrariness of this is flagrant. The phrase *they who were reputed* (*cf.* the Exposition of verses 2 and 6) is now supplied with its complement: *to be pillars.* Again Paul's intention is not to take away from the prestige of those three or to cast

---

[31] Important in this connection, too, is the absence of the article before ἀποστολήν. Hence every hint that Peter should be in possession of the true apostolate in distinction from the other apostles is carefully avoided.

[32] Some of the texts, however, have Πέτρος here also, presumably at the suggestion of verses 7 and 8.

doubt upon the legitimacy of their position. Paul wishes merely to indicate that they who in their special eminence had been played off against him were in fact in agreement with him (*cf.* the Exposition of verse 6). The giving of the right hands represents more than a reciprocal acknowledgment or testimony of friendship: it suggests rather a covenant.[33] The genitive *of fellowship* qualifies this settlement more precisely. It rested on reciprocal acknowledgment that all were partners in the same cause: belief in Christ, or, better, Christ Himself. This then was not a settlement in which the one is lording it over the other or imposing his will upon the other. Because of the fellowship which they acknowledged, they could arrive at a binding agreement. Thus something was ratified and solemnly approved, something that had already become a fact: namely, that the field of labor was to be divided. And thus the ministry of Paul and Barnabas was sanctioned. That was the important thing. The agreement was inclusive rather than exclusive: that is to say, it did not prevent Paul and Barnabas from working with Jews, and Peter and the others from working with the Gentiles; it meant, rather, that just as the last addressed themselves to the Jews, so it should be the privilege of Paul and Barnabas to preach the Gospel among the Gentiles.

10 What follows next is to be taken, not as the condition, but as the amplification of the agreement. It is to be taken as a request from one of the parties being made to the other. It was the one stipulation ("only") appended to the major agreement. By *the poor* Paul is recognizably referring to the poor at Jerusalem (*cf.* Rom. 15:26). Again and again we learn that the Gentile churches took up col-

---

[33] Compare also the following ἵνα. Δεξιὰ or δεξιαί can also simply mean *treaty,* or *compact,* because an exchange of right hands signified such. For proof-passages, see *e.g.,* Grundmann, TWNT, II, pp. 37-38, under δεξιός. Important, further, is the use of the third person ἔδωκαν, from which it is evident that the initiative was taken by the three.

lections for the church at Jerusalem (Rom. 15:25 ff., 1 Cor. 16:1 ff., 2 Cor. 8:1 ff., 9:1 ff., Acts 11:29 ff., 12:25, and 24:17).

The request for collections implies particularly difficult circumstances at Jerusalem (cf. 2 Cor. 8:14). In Acts 11:29 ff. the occasion for a collection was the serious famine under Claudius. Whether the consequences of that had not yet been overcome cannot be determined. It is likely, though, that by this means the thought, expressed by Paul in Romans 15:27, namely, that the Gentile churches had a certain material obligation to the church at Jerusalem, to be given in gratitude for the spiritual gift that it had given them, had found permanent lodging also with the leaders at Jerusalem, who accordingly came out in a plea for their poor. Paul explains in conclusion that he most particularly remembers this agreement,[34] and that he has carried it into effect[35] with a zealous energy.

It is deserving of remark that the apostle makes no mention here of the determinations of the apostolic council about which we read in Acts 15:23-29. He writes "only" of the help to the poor. On the basis of this fact, scholars have wanted to call the report of Acts 15 historically inaccurate on this point. If, however, we read the apostolic enactment of Acts 15 according to the so-called "Western" text, the difficulty diminishes. In that text, the enactment

---

[34] Compare the αὐτὸ τοῦτο.

[35] Some argue that the ἐσπούδασα must be taken to refer to what Paul was zealous to do at the apostolic conference, and that it thus constitutes an argument for the view that this conference coincided with Paul's visit to Jerusalem reported in Acts 11:29 ff. This assumption is unacceptable. The verb connotes an arduous exertion to which the apostle had to reconcile himself, and it seems unlikely that such ardor would be connected with the transfer of already collected funds. Then too the second clause would take away something of the rich significance of the visit introduced by ἵνα. The tense of the μνημονεύωμεν also suggests something permanent. And it is that permanent effort for the sake of the poor that the apostle is here confirming.

concerning "things strangled" is omitted, and the so-called "golden rule" is added. In that form there is not a single stipulation left that can be called typically Jewish or ceremonial; all that is left is some ethical principles, which already obtained in the Pauline churches, and required no mention as something new or special on this occasion. Still, we can hardly on this ground dismiss the form of the text of Acts 15 which most of the manuscripts give us. Even then, however, it remains a question in how far Paul regarded this enactment as something new, something therefore which restricted the freedom he preached (verse 4), and which therefore required mention at this time. We must not forget that the enactment of Acts 15 bears on freedom from ceremonial stipulations for the Gentiles, and that, as is evident also from other letters of Paul, the line of conduct recommended in the enactment was already being followed by Paul. It was, therefore, unnecessary for him to enter upon anything new because of the agreement named in this verse, except to be zealous in the matter of the collection.

PAUL RESISTS PETER AT ANTIOCH

2:11-21

11 But when Cephas came to Antioch, I resisted him to the face, because he stood condemned.

12 For before that certain came from James, he ate with the Gentiles; but when they came, he drew back and separated himself, fearing them that were of the circumcision.

13 And the rest of the Jews dissembled likewise with him; insomuch that even Barnabas was carried away with their dissimulation.

14 But when I saw that they walked not uprightly according to the truth of the gospel, I said unto Cephas before *them* all, If thou, being a Jew, livest as do the Gentiles, and not as do the Jews, how compellest thou the Gentiles to live as do the Jews?

15 We being Jews by nature and not sinners of the Gentiles,

16 yet knowing that a man is not justified by the works of the law but through faith in Jesus Christ, even we believed on Christ Jesus, that we might be justified by faith in Christ, and not by the works of the law: because by the works of the law shall no flesh be justified.

17 But if, while we sought to be justified in Christ, we ourselves also were found sinners, is Christ a minister of sin? God forbid.

18 For if I build up again those things which I destroyed, I prove myself a transgressor.

19 For I through the law died unto the law, that I might live unto God.

20 I have been crucified with Christ; and it is no longer I that live, but Christ liveth in me: and that *life* which I now live in the flesh I live in faith, *the faith* which is in the Son of God, who loved me, and gave himself up for me.

21 I do not make void the grace of God: for if righteousness is through the law, then Christ died for nought.

This portion corresponds directly with the foregoing, and serves to defend Paul's apostolic authority over against his challengers. At the same time it constitutes the transition to the grand central part of the letter in which the relationship of gospel and law is treated in full scope. In 1:12 ff. the apostle indicated that he had his commission not from men, but from God Himself, and that in receiving it he had been independent from the other apostles. In 2:1 ff. he pointed to the essential agreement between himself and the leaders at Jerusalem, implying that no one could play these off against him. Now, in 2:11 ff. he demonstrates that he stood so firmly grounded in the conviction of this gospel which he preached to the Gentiles that he had even in public contradicted Peter when the latter threatened to endanger the strength of that gospel. From all this Paul's opponents and the churches at Galatia may well conclude that Paul was not an upstart, self-promoted apostle to the Gentiles, but that on the contrary he could speak with full authority confirmed by his divine commission, his being in essential harmony with "Jerusalem," and his defense of the gospel even over against Peter.

The portion of the letter now in hand has always attracted considerable attention, and it has played an important role both in the history of the church and in that of exegetical research.[1] Very soon observers saw a certain threat to Peter's authority in the church in this part of the letter. So some commentators arrived at the construction that, not Simon Peter, but one of the seventy is here involved (so Clemens Alexandrinus and later Roman Catholics). Others have assumed that this disputation took place by arrangement among the apostles (so Hieronymus and later Roman Catholics). Such interpretations are sheer hypotheses and cannot be accepted. In Luther's life, too, this part of Paul's letter bulked very

---

[1] Compare Oepke, *op. cit.,* p. 49 ff.

large, both because of what is said in it concerning the
law, and because of Paul's public resistance to Peter. For
the Tübingen school (F. C. Baur, and others) these verses
constituted the *locus classicus* of their dialectical recon-
struction of original Christianity. Right up into the
modern period the hypothesis of the unreconcilable conflict between Paul and Peter has found new adherents
(among others, Ed. Schwarz, Ed. Meyer, and H. Lietzmann). Nowhere in the epistles, however, do we read
anything about such an antithesis — nor in the Acts. And
as for the data of this letter, Peter is not being presented
as essentially an opponent, but as a person who did not
have the courage of his convictions, and who, accordingly,
and apparently with the desired results, was set straight
by Paul.

11 Some want to fix the time of Peter's arrival as
preceding the apostolic council, on the ground that otherwise his performance at Antioch would not be intelligible.
Against this, it can be said that Peter could come to Antioch, where many Jews were certainly living, notwith-
standing the settlement of the council. Further, the
difference between Paul and Peter was concerned in the
first place, not with the way in which the Gentiles, but
with the way in which the Jews should conduct themselves. Although no time indication is given, it seems
to lie in the whole bearing of the context that Peter came
to Antioch *after* the apostolic council. Nothing is said
here about the purpose of Peter's coming. The original
of the word translated *I resisted* suggests a reaction to an
attack. It is as such that Paul regarded Peter's performance: as an attack upon the truth of the gospel. Hence
Paul resisted him without beating around the bush[2] and
in the presence of all[3] the witnesses. The words *because*

---

[2] κατὰ πρόσωπον.
[3] ἔμπροσθεν πάντων.

he stood condemned[4] presumably mean to suggest that Peter, by acting as he did, condemned himself.

12-13 These verses present the situation in outline. Peter had begun by eating with the Gentile Christians[5] and he kept this up for some time.[6] Eating with them presumably involves more than the celebration of communion. From 1 Cor. 11:20 it is apparent that the celebration of the Supper often coincided with the regular common feasts or meals. Besides, the expression used in verse 14, *to live as do the Gentiles,* has a wider reference. The Jewish regulations for going about with Gentiles were very strictly exacting, especially the rules of cleanness at meals. At first, that is, before *certain came from James,* Peter made no objection to a common fellowship with Gentiles on this score. The quoted words need not imply that these people came upon James' instigation,[7] nor that they were bent on regulating things at Antioch; the words tell us only that those who came were followers of James, and that they insisted on strict observation of the rules for the Jews. Right from the start, therefore, they apparently never participated in a meal with Gentile Christians. It was under the impetus of their presence that Peter *drew back and separated himself.* The first word[8] suggests an unobtrusive retreat. The second word indicates the result. Instead of fellowship, separation took place between Peter and the Gentile Christians. And the motive was the fear that the Jews would regard Peter as a transgressor of the law. Paul twice labels this attitude as dissembling, as hypocrisy: there was no inner conviction in it but only the adoption of a pose prompted by fear of

---

[4] κατεγνωσμένος: literally condemned, guilty; also translated: to be condemned, reprehensible.

[5] Such is the meaning of ἐθνῶν.

[6] As is evident from the imperfect tense.

[7] Presumably the ἀπὸ 'Ιακώβου goes with the τινες, and not with the ἐλθεῖν.

[8] ὑποστέλλειν: to retire.

others. This pusillanimity was true not only of Peter but also of the Jews who were at Antioch and who presumably acted as Peter acted before the arrival of James' followers. Of these Barnabas is specifically named. So strong was the tug of this hypocrisy[9] that even he who had, together with Paul, founded so many churches among the Gentiles, and certainly had eaten with them, now withdrew himself from eating with Gentile believers.

14 Paul first names the motive that prompted him to take exception to Peter and the others. Irrespective of what might have kept him from doing so, when he saw that the true, unmodified content of the gospel[10] was at stake, he did not scruple to oppose Peter in public. In so doing, he appealed to Peter's original attitude, to the time when Peter no longer observed the Jewish ethical code[11] in social contact with Gentiles. How could the man now, after such an attitude, again compel[12] the Gentile Christians to live as Jews? Such conduct would certainly prompt the Gentiles to try to live as Jews. Else there would be no room for them at one and the same table with the Jews, and they would remain in a position of inferiority. This first part of Paul's case therefore points out the inconsistency in Peter's conduct. Thereupon Paul argues directly from *the truth of the gospel.* He does not mention the decision that had been taken at Jerusalem. Still, that decision made for the same result. The moment Jews and Gentiles came together, the dilemma turned up again. Paul saw that very clearly in this situation. And he pointed it

---

[9] τῇ ὑποκρίσει: *in* or *through.*

[10] ἡ ἀλήθεια τοῦ εὐαγγελίου (compare the Exposition of verse 5). The ὀρθοποδεῖν used here occurs at no other point in the New Testament. ὀρθοποδοῦς: "on solid footing." The verb in this connection means about the same as: not wavering between two motives, resolutely heading for something. πρός constitutes the reference line, or point, according to which one can direct or orient himself.

[11] ἐθνικῶς and 'Ιουδαϊκῶς are here used in reference to the law.

[12] ἀναγκάζεις: *de conatu.*

out to Peter, apparently on the assumption that Peter would agree.

15-16 The problem whether the content of verses 15 and following is still being directed to Peter and is therefore part and parcel of the address delivered *before all* is difficult to answer with an unequivocal yes or no. Paul is here speaking from the viewpoint of Jewish Christians. It is natural to find the point of departure of this thought in the historical situation just described. That these next following words, however, are intended to be a report of what Paul said on that occasion, is another matter, and need not follow. We can easily picture Paul, beginning at verse 15, as speaking in a more general sense from the vantage point of Jewish Christians. Moreover, we hear nothing further in the sequel about the situation outlined in verse 14. Presumably we are not far from the truth, then, if we regard verses 15-21 as a transition from the historically occasioned to the generally considered aspects. The whole report of the incident at Antioch is after all presented for its illustrative significance. To what extent, however, we shall have to explain the next following verses in reference to verse 14, will become apparent as we proceed, especially in treating verse 17.

The force of verse 15 is concessive: "undoubtedly — we[13] are by nature Jews." Paul wants to detract nothing from that. The phrase *by nature* has reference here to the natural constitution of man as determined by descent and birth (*cf. e.g.,* Rom. 2:27). The other phrase, *sinners of the Gentiles,* is used to designate, not a particular category of people among the Gentiles, but the Gentiles in general. The word *sinners* as used here (and elsewhere — *cf.* Mt. 26:45) is synonymous with *Gentiles.* Paul is appropriating the current Jewish conception and linguistic practice.[14] In both there is reflected not only the Jewish sense

---

[13] ἡμεῖς: with special emphasis.
[14] Compare also Rengstorf, TWNT, I, p. 332, 329.

of privilege in possessing the Torah but also their self-esteem. What follows in verse 16, however, puts the concessive introductory clause in a singular light. For whatever the Jews might possess in privileged superiority to the Gentiles, they no more than the Gentiles could, on the basis of their privileged position, achieve a righteousness with God. That is the content of the Christian conviction to which Paul, without fear of contradiction, could and had to appeal over against Peter and over against his readers.[15] The *not justified* is used in the typically Pauline forensic sense. It expresses neither an ethical change or influence, nor an *iustum efficere* in the sense of causing someone to live a holy, unimpeachable life; it expresses, rather, the juridical judgment of God, in which man is protected from the sanction of the law in the judgment of God, and thus goes out acquitted. Accordingly, *by the works*[16] means about the same as on the basis of the works. At issue, in other words, is more than a human experience: at issue is God's verdict. And such an emancipating verdict is impossible for man, whoever he be, on the basis of the works of the law. There is but[17] one way and one means: that of faith in Jesus Christ. Thus the basis for the justification is sought in Jesus Christ, and faith is the means by which[18] man has communion with Christ and

---

[15] εἰδότες.

[16] ἐξ ἔργων νόμου, without articles; hence qualitative. One can interpret the genitive as the works "demanded by the law" or as the works "accomplished by the law."

[17] ἐὰν μή really means "save," or "except," and announces an exception. Here, however, it must be interpreted as an absolute (not merely as a partial) contrast to the preceding. The ASV has only *but*.

[18] The διὰ πίστεως is interchangeable with ἐκ πίστεως: verse 16b (*cf.* Rom. 3:26, 30, 5:1, Gal. 3:8, 11, 24, and 5:5). It is also interchangeable with πίστει (Rom. 3:28), and with ἐπὶ τῇ πίστει (Phil. 3:9), but at no point with διὰ πίστιν. Faith is not presented as the ground for justification.

shares in His gifts (*cf.* verse 19 ff.) This faith can at one time be regarded as the means or instrument through which, at another time as the organ out of which, the justification comes. In this way, however, the emphasis is always upon the fact that the justification comes to man not from his works, not from something in himself, but from his relationship with Christ.

The second part of the predication of verse 16 reminds the Jewish Christians, who are all along involved in the reference of the sentence, that (*even*) they,[19] irrespective of their special privileges, believed[20] on Jesus Christ in order to be justified. The repetition of all these concepts drives home the more forcefully the truth that for the Jews also there is no other way. And this truth is finally confirmed still further by the concluding words of verse 16, in which Paul refers to an utterance in Psalm 143:2. True, the words, *by the works of the law,* cannot be found in Psalm 143. But this does not rob the reference of its force. In that Psalm the poet gives expression in as general a form as possible to the consciousness that no living man[21] can be justified before God. This implies that the Psalmist did not expect the justification to accrue to the works of the law either. Hence, the negative phase of the "not through works, but through faith alone" was nothing new, since it already lay contained in the genuine sense of guilt of the Old Testament saints. Later Judaism had however fallen away from this profoundly religious sense of guilt.

---

[19] καὶ ἡμεῖς.

[20] ἐπιστεύσαμεν: ingressive aorist.

[21] οὐ . . . πᾶσα σαρξ. οὐ . . . πᾶσα is Hebraic (*cf.* Mt. 24:22); σάρξ designates in the most general possible way the human, creaturely life. Elsewhere it sometimes designates pregnantly the *sinful* human nature (*cf.* 5:16 ff.). In this usage, the σάρξ lacks that pregnant significance, although undoubtedly the thought that all men are sinners also lies at the basis of the whole statement.

17 The immediately preceding verses were easy to understand as issuing from the situation described in verse 14. Now, however, there follows an objection, perhaps not so much derived from the occasional event at Antioch (it would, *e.g.,* be difficult to put the objection in Peter's mouth), but an objection which inevitably shines through every preaching of the justification by faith (*cf.* Rom. 6:1, 15), and one which is apparently raised here in special relevancy to the readers of this letter. The objection has reference to the seeming ethical danger of the doctrine. Does it not make for godless and normless living? The objection begins by saying something that cannot be denied:[22] if even we (Jews) ourselves, quite as much as the Gentiles, are found to be sinners,[23] and there is, therefore, no essential difference between those who observe the law and the sinners of the Gentiles... And thence the question which, on the basis of that clause, can be asked, and is as a matter of fact always being asked anew: Is this Christ, then,[24] a minister of sin, serving in its cause? The answer could not be more definitely negative.[25] Paul nowhere does injustice to the gravity of sin or to the holiness of the law. Both are always totally assumed.

---

[22] εἰ—: *siquidem.* It introduces, not a contrary to fact, nor a potential, but a condition of fact (*cf. e.g.,* Col. 3:1).

[23] *Inasmuch as* or *because* (ζητοῦντες) we seek to be justified in Christ. The "seeking" does not suggest that we are unsure of the success, but points rather to the desire and the hope of the believers. ἐν Χριστῷ now clearly indicates that the justification of the believers takes place in Christ. The point is not only that He constitutes the ground of the justification: He is also the person in whom as Head of the covenant the act of justification takes place.

[24] ἄρα is a concluding adverb. It can also, however, be taken as an interrogative particle, and so be left untranslated (*cf.* the translation); however, we cannot be sure whether this use occurs elsewhere in Paul's writings. Whether or not we are dealing here with a question is not, of course, in dispute.

[25] μὴ γένοιτο is the equivalent of the Hebrew חְלִילָה לִי

18 The significance of verse 18 in the logical context is very obscure — a fact which has given rise to all sorts of explanations, and also has its repercussion for the exposition of verse 17. Very plain is the fact that the predications *I build up* and *I destroyed* refer to the building up and the breaking down of self-righteousness on the basis of the works of the law.[26] Peter, apparently, had done this: first he had trusted in Christ and thus broken down his own righteousness. Later, apparently, he again[27] wanted to build it up. Nevertheless the bearing of the remark is undoubtedly wider than that. The apostle has in mind also and especially the situation among the Galatians, who, in a far graver sense than Peter, were also engaged in building up what they had first surrendered. Paul speaks here in the supra-individual first person.[28] He wants to make the *matter* plain, rather than to aim at this or that person. Hence, the question becomes: What is meant by *I prove myself*[29] *a transgressor,* and how are we in connection with that to understand the progress of the argument? As we see it, the whole statement of verse 18 should be

---

[26] The words καταλύειν and οἰκοδομεῖν are words derived from the work of building (*cf.* Mark 14:58). The reference of the predication is not to the law itself: for this use of καταλύειν one may compare Mt. 5:17. οἰκοδομεῖν can hardly take the law as its object. Concerning justification, which rests on the law, it can be said, however, that it is broken down and built up, when conceived of as the ground of salvation.

[27] πάλιν: that is, as he had before, when he did not yet live out of faith.

[28] The clause introduced by εἰ announces a potential this time, precisely because Paul is not now speaking for himself, but in using the first person has others (Peter, the Galatians) in mind.

[29] The συνιστάνω with the double accusative is difficult to translate: to constitute someone something; with the ἐμαυτόν it becomes: to prove oneself something or someone, or, really, to recommend or present oneself as such.

taken as a further explanation of the *God forbid* in verse 17.[30] In our opinion, this is possible if we construe the sense of the passage as follows: When a person returns from the point of view of faith to that of the law, he is only increasing his sin. In other words, he is demonstrating anew that he cannot keep the law. Hence a return from faith does not mean a diminution of sin at all, but rather a renewed surrender to it. And verse 19 will indicate what faith in Christ means. In this way verse 18 can be regarded as (the beginning of) a further illumination of 17b. It is as such, too, that the causal *for* introduces it.

19 In verse 19 the argument is continued. Further cause is shown why faith in Christ cannot be a ministering of sin. So Paul illustrates how he,[31] precisely by expecting nothing from the law, leaves the way open to live *unto God,* and so emerges from the status of *being a transgressor.* This, then, at the same time goes to show how appropriate the "God forbid" of verse 17 was.

The apostle contrasts the living unto God with the dying unto the law. By the first term of the contrast is meant the God-directed, God-consecrated life. The possi-

---

[30] Others see in verse 18 a more specific illumination of the question asked in verse 17, and they put this verse also, so to speak, in the mouth of Peter and the other legalistic Christians. The logical context would then run as follows: "Do you suppose that when we seek our justification in Christ, Christ is a minister of sin? Surely that is a thought that must be entirely repudiated. Still you seem attracted to the idea, *for* when you now again build up what you first broke down, you obviously repudiate your first course of action." As we see it, this interpretation is hardly plausible in view of the position of μὴ γένοιτο. After these words, one no longer expects in verse 18 a further explanation of the question asked in 17a; what one expects, rather, is an explanation of its rejection as demanded by 17b.

[31] This ἐγώ is also to be regarded as representative, not as individually specified.

bility of living thus was, however, given him only after he had died to the law. This being dead to the law implies two things: (a) his own impotent ethical condition, and (b) his unprofitableness with regard to the law.[32] The law can no longer use him. He is what a dead servant would be to his master. However, there is a certain irony in this development too. For, he got into this condition of death, in which he is producing nothing for the law, *through the law.* The law has put him to death for its service, whipped him to death, so to speak, by its demands. It is the same thought as that of 2 Cor. 3:6 (*cf.* also Gal. 3:21). The thrust is that the law is in no position to give man what it demands[33] of him. All it can do is to demand, to forbid, to judge, and to condemn. So it is that man dies *through* the law: he is beaten to death by it and falls into God's judgment. That, then, is not the fault of the law, but of the sinner. The law cannot save, quicken, but only slay the sinner. And this death Paul has now died so *that* he might live unto God. This is again not to say that this God-consecrated life was Paul's purpose or his plan, nor that the law had this in mind or granted it; but the factual result is described all the same as a *purpose* because in this way another power came to master him, and he could proceed to live unto God. We are told about that power in the sequel. In this first part of verse 19 Paul speaks — and this is characteristic of the whole letter to the Galatians — about the law in a negative sense. We are not warranted, however, in drawing wrong conclusions from that, as though Paul did not regard the law as a holy thing (*cf. e.g.,* 5:14). The issue in this whole matter is not about the law as norm but about the law as a life-principle and a life-potential, namely, for serving God. The law cannot give sinful man that potentiality.

---

[32] The νόμῳ is to be taken as a dative *incommodi,* just as Θεῷ clearly is a dative *commodi* (*cf.* 2 Cor. 5:15 and Rom. 6:11).

[33] Compare also Gutbrod, TWNT, IV, p. 1067.

20-21 In the Greek text the *Christ* is placed at the very beginning of this passage. Thus the apostle begins to point out how the life unto God has become possible in him. So the thought that Christ should be the minister of sin turns out to be the very opposite of the truth. For the life unto God is precisely the thing that is determined by Christ, and issues from communion with Him.[34] True, this communion is first of all a communion in *death*. In order to cause His own to live, Christ first had to subject Himself to the power and the curse of the law, and to surrender Himself to these (*cf.* 3:13). At the same time, however, the possibility of escape from the curse and the death of the law issues from the death of Christ (*cf.* Rom. 7:4).

Paul uses the perfect tense in speaking of his having died with Christ, that is, in speaking of something that once took place and has not lost its power since. This thing that has happened somewhere else in the past does not refer to Paul's subjective experience, but to the death of Christ. The believers, by virtue of their corporate belonging to Him, were included in that dying. Of course, this communion in death materializes subjectively also in the believers, and that precisely is what baptism signifies and seals (Rom. 6:3); in communion with the death of Christ, the believers die to sin, so that its lordship is broken and the freedom of the life unto God is born. It is this life which is now more specifically described: *and it is no longer I that live, but Christ liveth in me.* Obviously this is not a psychological or biological utterance. Paul himself, too, is still living in a certain sense (*cf.* verse 20b). Rather, the utterance says something about the existential determination of life. This it is which springs no longer from Paul's natural self, but from Christ. This determi-

---

[34] According to Nestle's arrangement of verses, the words Χριστῷ συνεσταύρωμαι still belong to verse 19.

nation is so overwhelming that one can say: *Christ lives in me.* Verse 20b explains the life unto God in Christ more particularly: The life that I now (that is, after having died with Christ) live in the flesh (that is, in the human temporality of this life) I live in faith in the Son of God. Such is not to say that *Christ lives in me* is the same as *I live in faith.* The first term gives expression to the new redemptive status of the believers — the result of being included in Christ's death and resurrection. It means also that Christ and His redemption break through into the life of His own by means of His Spirit, and that so Christ lives *in* them. So they are liberated from the curse as well as from the power of sin, and so their life can be a life *unto God.* Seen from their side, that life is a life in faith, a consciously Christ-oriented life. And in faith the communion with Christ is also exercised by the believers. From the objective side, this faith is called a faith in the Son of God. So the glory and the power of Christ and of His self-surrender and love are pointed out. Faith in this wonderful, divine love, and the being taken into this love — it is that which redeems life and sets it free. The aorists point to the historical fact of Christ's loving self-sacrifice. That constitutes the ground for faith in this love. But He who loved thus also lives *in* His own. Hence the life of faith in Him is not a matter merely of being oriented to what has happened, but is also a new, reborn life, in which the strength of Christ's love, in which the liberating Spirit, reveals Himself.

Those last words redirect our thought to the subject of whether there is room for anything else alongside of this faith. Verse 21 excludes that possibility: I do not make void the grace of God. Whatever others may want to do . . . not *I.* And that is precisely what I should be doing if I again began to rely on the works of the law. Then Christ would not have had to die (*cf.* 5:11). His death on the cross is at stake. At its profoundest that was the essence of the controversy with Peter. And that is the consequence of what the Galatians are doing also, if they again permit themselves to be brought under the law. That, too, is the thing that will be sharply and forcefully said in the sequel, beginning immediately at 3:1.

PART TWO

The Gospel of Justification By Faith Alone Maintained Over Against the Judaizer's Challenge

3:1-5:12

Now the apostle arrives at the point of defending the gospel in the general sense of the word and of fully unfolding his thoughts. His argument is full of power and is dynamically charged. It does not follow a carefully plotted scheme of treatment. The forward movement of the thought takes a natural course, and, despite its profundity, the argument is easy to follow.

CHAPTER III

AN APPEAL TO THE GALATIANS' EXPERIENCE OF FAITH

3:1-5

1 O foolish Galatians, who did bewitch you, before whose eyes Jesus Christ was openly set forth crucified?

2 This only would I learn from you, Received ye the Spirit by the works of the law, or by the hearing of faith?

3 Are ye so foolish? having begun in the Spirit, are ye now perfected in the flesh?

4 Did ye suffer so many things in vain? if it be indeed in vain.

5 He therefore that supplieth to you the Spirit, and worketh miracles among you, *doeth he it* by the works of the law, or by the hearing of faith?

1 For the first time since 1:11, Paul addresses his readers by name. He refers to them now, not as brethren, but as Galatians, placing them, so to speak, at a formal distance in order to summon them to their responsibility. The tone of his words is passionate. All that had been said in the foregoing about the excellence of Christ is apparently on the point of being denied by the Galatians. One would think they had been charmed or bewitched. Naturally the apostle does not mean this in the literal sense. But he puts the thing thus forcefully in order to show them the measure of their spiritual folly,[1] and to startle them into reflection. With what clarity and power the preaching of the gospel had been brought them! And in that preaching the reliance upon their own works of

---

[1] ἀνόητος: it means *unthinkable,* but in the active sense also *foolish, unwise* (verse 3, Luke 24:25, Rom. 1:14, and other places). The reference is not so much to a lack of intelligence as to a mistaken use of it.

the law had been laid bare in all its hopelessness (*cf.* 2:20 ff.). The use of the participle *crucified* tells of something that has been accomplished and is now settled, and the reference in this connection is not so much to the fact as to the fruit of Christ's being crucified. The word translated *openly set forth* is not to be taken as a plastic representation of the suffering and death of Christ, but rather — the Greek word indicates it[2] — as a public announcement, a proclamation, in which the validity of a particular fact or a particular condition is proclaimed. True, the phrase *before whose eyes* tells of the graphic quality, the visibility of the content in the preaching, but this, presumably, points less to the portraiture of Christ's suffering than to the lucidity and unmistakability of the preaching.

2 In a flourish of moving rhetoric, the apostle says that there is only one thing which he would still like to learn from them. For the rest he does not want to hear anything from them in their folly. The answer to this one last question is in principle determinative of the issue between them and him. Their own witness must convince them of their error. To that end Paul reminds them of the time of their conversion and of their receiving of the gift of the Spirit. We are to think of those special operations of the Spirit by which in the early period of the Christian church the acceptance of the gospel was sometimes accompanied and confirmed (verse 5; *cf.* also Acts 8:14-17, 10:44-46, and 19:6). The apostle refers his readers to this, because the receiving of the gift of the Spirit is surely the most unmistakable evidence of God's favor and the plainest guarantee of eternal redemption. This being so, from what source and along which way had these gifts come to them: by the works of the law or by the hearing of faith? If they could answer that, they could also figure

---

[2] προγράφειν: see besides G. Schrenk, TWNT, I, pp. 771-772, under γράφω, also G. Milligan, *Here and There among the Papyri*, 1923, p. 78.

out whether or not they were now on the right path. For the expression *the works of the law,* see the Exposition of 2:16. Opposed to it is the expression *the hearing of faith,*[3]

[3] The translation is not easy to manage, inasmuch as ἀκοή as well as πίστις can be used in both an active and a passive sense. Further, ἀκοή can in the active sense designate either the organ of hearing, the capacity of hearing (Mt. 13:24, Mark 17:35, and the like) or the act of hearing itself (as, presumably in Rom. 10:17). In the passive sense, ἀκοή means tidings or news (Mt. 4:24, 14:1, and 24:6), and it so becomes the technical designation for the preaching (John 12:38, Rom. 10:16, 1 Thess. 2:13, and Heb. 4:2). Since ἀκοή occurs in this last sense most frequently, and since it is doubtful, even, whether the act of "hearing" is intended by any New Testament word, one is inclined to take ἀκοή in the passive sense here also. The difficulty then arises from its connection with τῆς πίστεως. True, πίστις occurs in the New Testament in the sense of the content of faith, the *fides quae creditur* (e.g., Jude 3, 20); one could therefore take the πίστεως as the object of the preaching (ἀκοή). But this meaning of πίστις is, compared with the subjective sense of *fides qua creditur,* extremely rare. Only, this subjective sense of πίστις fits in badly with the passive, objective sense of ἀκοῆς. We could, then, translate the word as "preaching of the gospel," and interpret it as a preaching "which has faith as its object." As we see it, however, this is not a convincing version. Another possibility is to take the ἀκοή in a passive sense, and the πίστις in an active one, and then to associate the ἐξ with πίστεως, not with ἀκοῆς. That would result in the version: by way of faith in what was heard, namely the preaching. That makes good sense, but runs into the difficulty that it does not correspond linguistically to ἐξ ἔργων νόμου. All these difficulties arise from taking ἀκοῆς in the passive sense. An active significance is therefore very appealing. The result would then be *the hearing of faith,* and one could still choose between the view which accepts the πίστεως as a subjective genitive, and that which takes it as a qualitative genitive: in other words, "the hearing of faith," or "the faithful hearing." The main decision, however, is that of ἀκοή as *preaching* (preaching of the faith) and ἀκοή as *hearing* (faithful or believing hearing). We choose for the second of these alternatives, partly also because it corresponds best with the first term of the contrast. If we were to take ἀκοή as meaning *preaching,* the first term of the contrast would presumably also have been given out differently (for example, as *preaching of the law* rather than as *works of the law*). Certainly the active sense of ἀκοή corresponds best with *works of the law,* irrespective of whether πίστεως is then taken as a subjective genitive, as in the translation being followed here, or as a qualitative one. The omission of the articles serves to stress the qualitative aspect.

the hearing of the gospel, that is, the believing appropriation of the redemption wrought by Christ — the hearing, most especially, of the gospel of the cross (verse 1).

3 Nothing further is said about the answer which Paul expects to the question asked in verse 2. That is not necessary. It is self-evident. From that point, then, the apostle chides his readers for their foolishness. He further characterizes this folly by way of asking a question. The question contains a double contrast in chiastic form: beginning in the Spirit, ending in the flesh. The first term refers to the time when the Galatians came to the faith. Then they had made a new beginning *through* or *in* (the sphere, the communion of) the Spirit. Now they were busy seeking the completion of that beginning, and seeking it in the flesh. By *flesh* in this connection is meant the human nature in itself, the human without the divine. The word is not opposed at this point to the Spirit in the same way as in 5:16 ff. (as the principle of sin distinguished from the saving power of the Spirit), but as the self-oriented human nature in distinction from the strength and power of God. Paul brings the law and the flesh into relationship with each other here because the law has its bearing upon all sorts of physical conditions and activities: upon circumcision, for instance, to which the churches of Galatia were succumbing again (*cf.* 6:13). That was the tragic end of the glorious beginning. They were engaged in falling back from the divine power of the Spirit into the impotence of man. Not without irony Paul denominates this progress with an inclusive term:[4] Are ye now *perfected,* he asks, perhaps because the heretical teachers used this word, as though the thing they were recommending were the loftiest manifestation of the life unto God.

---

[4] ἐπιτελεῖσθε.

4 According to the ASV,[5] the apostle brings up yet another argument. It is an argument borrowed from what the churches had *suffered* as Christians and by virtue of their loyalty to the gospel. Paul asks whether they had previously experienced all these things in vain — inasmuch as they now deny the faith. Had this been their intent all along, they would not have had to subject themselves to oppression and persecution (*cf.* 1:10, 5:11). The words *in vain* are, however, overtaken and called back: *if it be indeed in vain.* Some commentators think that by this means the apostle wants to soften somewhat the effect of what he has said. A cast of doubt would then be thrown over the question of whether the Galatians had suffered in vain: "if at least — as I hope not — it was in vain." However, a different interpretation seems more acceptable to us, according to which 4b represents an intensification rather than a mitigation of 4a. According to this view, Paul is really saying: "if indeed *in vain* is strong enough to suggest what it is." The point is not merely that they are losing the fruit of the suffering which they once bore: they — who were tried and appointed to suffer as Christians — must fear that their denial of this suffering will be reckoned to them as guilt, and the blessing

---

[5] We may well question whether this translation of the ASV is accurate. For ἐπάθετε can also be translated *did ye undergo, or experience,* and be understood as applying to the operations of the Spirit mentioned in verses 2, 3, and 5. True, the first translation is the more current one. The objections to the first amount to this, however, that the whole context, also the summarizing verse 5, says nothing at all about suffering or persecution, anymore than does the sequel of the letter. All the same, τοσαῦτα points to something immediately present in the minds of the writer and the readers. There is good deal, then, that pleads for the view that this word also refers to the frequently reiterated gift of the Spirit. The verb πάσχειν can serve to designate that these gifts, quite beyond the achievement of the readers on any other basis, had fallen to them, overwhelmed them, quite apart from their own doing. Such an interpretation also suits the exposition of εἴ γε καὶ εἰκῇ given in the text above.

be converted into curse. The past must do more than put them into a different frame of thought. It will also, if they persist in their present deflection, constitute them as guilty.

5 Once more the question asked in verse 2 is repeated.[6] The readers must not try to shy away from answering it. They must make a commitment on this, and conduct themselves accordingly. This time the question is put in the third, not in the second person, in order to drive the seriousness of it home the more forcefully. For *He that supplieth*[7] *to*[8] *you the Spirit* . . . is God, even though His name is not mentioned. Hence that thing which they once received as a gift[9] has become a determinative norm for the truth of the gospel. And that is why the responsibility under which the Galatians are placed is so great and serious.

---

[6] The οὖν summarizes, recapitulates, and lays what has been said once more upon the mind and conscience of the readers. This recapitulation also pleads for the view that verse 4 refers to an experience of the gifts of the Spirit.

[7] ἐπιχορηγῶ: to pay for the costs of a choir; hence, in general: to give. The ἐπί intensifies it: hence, *abundantly supply.*

[8] ὑμῖν can also have the meaning: *among you.*

[9] This gift is now more specifically described as the divine operation (ἐνεργῶν) of forces (δυνάμεις), be it exclusively as spiritual gifts, or also as miracles of healing, and the like.

THIS EXPERIENCE IN HARMONY WITH SCRIPTURE

3:6-9

6 Even as Abraham believed God, and it was reckoned unto him for righteousness.

7 Know therefore that they that are of faith, the same are sons of Abraham.

8 And the scripture, foreseeing that God would justify the Gentiles by faith, preached the gospel beforehand unto Abraham, *saying,* In thee shall all the nations be blessed.

9 So then they that are of faith are blessed with the faithful Abraham.

Paul is now going to demonstrate that not only the experience of the Galatians, but that the Scriptures also, most especially what these have to say about Abraham, confirm the answer he expected from his readers in what he has said before. Very probably his opponents, too, had in their efforts made an appeal to Abraham. From the fact that Paul in the next following verses gives a definition of "children of Abraham," we may, perhaps, infer that the opponents had tried to show on the basis of Scripture that it was necessary to be a child of Abraham in order to share in the salvation of the Lord. And, as they construed it, that meant circumcision, and the observation of the law.

6 By his phrase *even as Abraham,* the apostle wants to contend that what the Galatians might have known on the basis of their experience (verses 1-5) is in accord with what the Scriptures have to say about Abraham. This was not a matter merely of agreement. The appeal to

Abraham was an appeal to an exceptionally authoritative example.[1] Abraham, after all, was the father of Israel. He stood at the beginning of the history of redemption, in so far as it affected Israel. With him God had made the Covenant. And of him Scripture,[2] the divine norm for faith and life, says that God reckoned his faith unto him for righteousness. By this faith is meant the spiritual disposition with which Abraham responded to the promise given him by God. The apostle sets this faith in the foreground as the real, governing principle of Abraham's life. The rabbis, too, have devoted attention to Abraham's faith, and interpreted it as the moving force in his life. However, they have again and again spun it into the texture of their nomistic conceptions. So the faith got to be an accomplishment on Abraham's part which gave him the right to reward. In Gen. 15 this faith is described as Abraham's readiness to surrender unreservedly to the word of the Lord, regardless of how incredible it seemed. Paul interprets it in opposition to *works,* that is to say, as an unreserved, exclusive trust in the grace of God, accompanied by a renouncement of all pretensions borrowed from the works of the law. Unquestionably, the concept of faith is more specialized in this connection than it is in Gen. 15, where the opposition, faith *versus* works, does not come into view. All the same, the center of gravity in both places is the trust in God's work, without consideration of what is attainable by human strength, and possible to it. In Gen. 15 the *reckon unto*[3] refers to the free and favorable dispensation of God by which He accounted Abraham's faith to him for righteousness. In the later Jewish theology this accounting is represented as a credit

---

[1] The idea of a norm or measure is contained in καθώς.

[2] Genesis 15:6, quoted here according to LXX.

[3] λογίζεσθαι εἰς is used in profane Greek as a commercial term meaning *to appraise* or *assess*. It is found here, as in LXX, as a translation of the Hebrew חשב plus the double objective, and means: to reckon, credit, or account.

entry in heaven for a humanly merited earning.[4] Paul conceives of the idea in a radically different way, as is evident also from Rom. 4:3 ff. There he illuminates the difference between to reckon *as of grace* and to reckon *as of debt,* and then goes on to show that Gen. 15 has nothing to do with the last kind of reckoning. Hence the meaning here too must be *to reckon as of grace*: a divine judgment, therefore, which depends, not upon human merit, but upon God's favorable dispensation. The *righteousness* here designated is not an ethical property, but a divinely conferred quality, by reason of which he is free of guilt and punishment. Negatively it means: being placed outside the state of guilt; and positively: to be in harmony with the divine standard of judgment. Such justification has not at all an arbitrary character. The big assumption underlying it is that God accomplished the punishment which His righteousness demands in Christ on the cross, and that by being included in Christ the believer can arrive at acquittal.

7 The conclusion which Paul draws in this verse from Gen. 15 is presented to his readers as something plain and irrefutable, and as one which they must now once and for all make their own. This conclusion concerns the question, Who are children of Abraham? It may be that the Judaizers had also operated with this question. After all, the promise was to Abraham's seed (Gen. 17:7). Paul points out that this descent from Abraham is not determined by physical descent, nor by circumcision, but by spiritual kinship with Abraham. What matters is the inner oneness. *They that are of faith*: the people who believe, the believers[5] — they are kin to Abraham (*cf.*

---

[4] Compare, *e.g.*, H. W. Heidland, TWNT, IV, p. 293, under λογίζομαι.

[5] οἱ ἐκ πίστεως: ἐκ "The preposition describes source, yet not source of being — they do not owe their existence to faith — but source of character and standing, existence after a certain manner," Burton, *op. cit.*, p. 155.

2:12). Faith is therefore the criterion for being sons of Abraham. The statement is emphatic: *the same are the sons of Abraham.* In this verse Paul maintains to the full the unity of the old and new covenants. The promise made to Abraham still holds. The method by which it is obtained is faith. The fact that natural descent and being incorporated into Abraham's seed by circumcision also has its significance does not come into consideration; elsewhere it is expressly acknowledged, also by Paul (Rom. 9:4; *cf.* Acts 2:39). But not by this is the true covenant-community determined, and the Galatians must come to acknowledge that.

8 Paul goes a step further. He says that kinship with Abraham, and the blessing connected with it, depends on faith, that therefore the Gentiles can share in it, and — this is the further step — that this can not only be indirectly inferred from the Scripture, but is expressly stated in it. *The scripture* is personified at this point. Really God Himself is being designated, for His word to Abraham is cited, and His foresight determined this utterance. It is Scripture, however, which, so to speak, preserves this word of God alive and makes it available. The apostle is alluding to the blessing of God pronounced upon Abraham in Gen. 12:3. When this pronouncement came to Abraham the blessing itself was still quite entirely a future matter. And the way in which it would be realised, namely, the way of justification by faith, was not yet visible. Still, it all lay contained in the word of God addressed to Abraham, as is now (Paul means to say) evident. Nor was this accidental. It was the divine foreknowledge that accomplished this.

Paul finds these things designated in the words: *in thee shall all the nations be blessed.* Plainly the sharing of all the nations in Abraham's blessing cannot be based upon biological relationship with him. Hence the apostle sees the evidence in these words of the fact that the Gentiles will be saved in the way of faith. One can ask; of course, to what extent this meaning was also in the mind of the writer and the first reader of the Book of Genesis. But the main thing remains what the Scripture, as the Word of God, intended. And this becomes evident in the fulfillment of God's revelation and promise as pointed out by Paul.

The promise made to Abraham is here qualified as being the gospel. The citation itself is a combination of Gen. 12:3[6] (cf. Gen. 28:14) and Gen. 18:18 (cf. 22:18 and 26:4). The blessing in question here does not affect material welfare only but also the whole curse which lies upon the human race. In[7] Abraham this curse will be lifted from all mankind.

9 This verse recapitulates that the Scripture of Gen. 12:3 permits no other conclusion than the one formulated in verse 8a. How else could the Gentiles be blessed together with Abraham save in the communion of faith? Of works of the law, in the sense in which the heretical teachers spoke of them, there was nothing at all in Abraham. For him too, the promise preceded the circumcision (cf. Rom. 4:9, 10). Not as a circumcised Abraham, or as an Abraham loyal to the law, did he receive the promise — the promise also for the nations. In that there lies a clear indication of the way in which the nations, too, share in the blessing.

---

[6] It is true that some think the *niphal* of Gen. 12:3 must be used as a reflexive: to bless oneself, to call oneself blessed. This would then be intended to carry the implication that the enjoyment of unusual favor would be indicated by the proverb "As fortunate as Abraham." This can hardly be right, however, because in Gen. 12 the issue is precisely what God will do to Abraham and all nations. The positive meaning which Paul also sees in this word has most to recommend it.

[7] In verse 8 the ἐν is used to designate the kinship with Abraham; in verse 9 σύν is used, but without difference of meaning.

THE LAW CANNOT SUPPLY THE PROMISED SALVATION

3:10-14

10 For as many as are of the works of the law are under a curse: for it is written, Cursed is everyone who continueth not in all things that are written in the book of the law, to do them.

11 Now that no man is justified by the law before God, is evident: for, The righteous shall live by faith;

12 and the law is not of faith; but, He that doeth them shall live ·in them.

13 Christ redeemed us from the curse of the law, having become a curse for us; for it is written, Cursed is every one that hangeth on a tree:

14 that upon the Gentiles might come the blessing of Abraham in Christ Jesus; that we might receive the promise of the Spirit through faith.

10-12 In these verses the apostle confirms (*for*) what has gone before by an argument *e contrario*. First he has pointed out from Scripture that righteousness is by way of faith. Now he proceeds to show, again by an appeal to Scripture, that righteousness cannot be by way of the law. To that end he establishes the point that all who seek their justification out[1] of the works of the law in reality lie under the curse,[2] quite the opposite of Abraham's blessing.

---

[1] ὅσοι . . . ἐξ ἔργων νόμου εἰσίν, by analogy with οἱ ἐκ πίστεως in verse 7. ἐκ serves to characterize. For comment on the genitive νόμου, see the Exposition of 2:16.

[2] ὑπὸ κατάραν is used without the article, the more sharply to enhance the contrast with εὐλογία of verses 8 and 9. The ὑπό makes of the κατάρα a real power which reigns and brings devastation upon those subjected to it. The curse is the sovereign utterance of the living God, effective, charged with power.

In substantiation of this Paul cites Deut. 27:26.[3] In that passage all those who do not fulfill the demands of the law in all respects are placed under the curse. Further, the fact that Scripture recognizes no way to be justified by the works of the law becomes apparent also from the saying of Habakkuk 2:4: The righteous shall live by faith. The law, on the contrary, does not speak of faith, of believing, but of doing. Hence, those are going counter to Scripture who expect justification from the works of the law. Such is the argument in verses 10-12. The reference to Deut. 27:26 in verse 10 is not motivated further. The assumption is that there is someone who "continueth in all things that are written in the book of the law." It has been remarked that the original sense of Deut. 27:26 does not proceed from this assumption, that it does not aim to bring all people under the curse, but wishes rather to summon men to a meticulously careful obedience to the law. Such certainly is the case. But this is not to deny, of course, that this formulation (*who continueth not in all things...*) taken strictly, that is to say, according to the absolute norm — such as, for instance, Jesus lays down in Matt. 5:21-48 — knocks the bottom out of every hope of being saved on the basis of the works of the law. As for the difference of intention between the use of this passage here and in Deut. 27, we ought not to forget that the whole development of Jewish legalism lies between Deut. 27 and Gal. 3. In that development the basis of salvation was shifted more and more from divine grace to human merit. If in the sphere of grace, therefore, Deut. 27:26 can have a positive significance, namely, to bind the reverencing of the law of God upon the hearts of His graciously favored covenant-people, in the sphere of merit Deut. 27:26 can mean only the curse. It is out of that last sphere of meaning that Paul is arguing, his

---

[3] Partly according to LXX. The δέ of verse 11 is not adversative but connective only.

eye, the whole while, of course, being on his opponents. The very thing that had been for Israel, so long as it lived out of grace, an impetus to living a life of grateful obedience to God, meant for those who looked to human merit for the fulfillment of expectation the end of all hope]— this according to the absolute norm, by which God judges.

And as for the reference to Habakkuk 2:4 in verse 11, that passage is one of the few Old Testament examples in which faith is presented as the one thing necessary for redemption.[4] In Habakkuk 2:4 this faith is not set in contrast to the works of the law, however, but over against the arrogance and self-confidence of the wicked. Positively seen, though, the faith intended in Hab. 2 and Gal. 3 is essentially the same. It is a resting in God without regard to human care and effort. In the quotation, the word the *righteous* is not used in a specific juridical sense.[5] The question is not how a man shall become righteous, but how the righteous (the pious) shall *live*, in the full and deep sense of an unafraid and unthreatened life — hence, in relationship also to the divine punishment.

In verse 12, finally, we find the reference to Lev. 18:5. It gives us the condition which the *law* lays down for life, namely, to keep the commandments, and so demonstrates

---

[4] Sometimes Hab. 2:4 is translated to mean that the righteous, in contrast to the faithless wicked, "shall live by virtue of his faith (loyalty)." And, as a matter of fact, the Hebrew word, for which πίστις is used here, does generally mean: loyalty, trustworthiness. According to the context (Hab. 2:3), it should refer here to a faithful steadfastness over against God and His word: in short, to faith. The LXX translates as follows: *My* faithfulness, that is, of Jahwe. Later rabbinical thought seized on this passage and made it serviceable to a doctrine of merit by construing *faith* as the monotheistic confession.

[5] δίκαιος: a person who, judging by his conduct, stands in the right relationship to God; pious.

the incompatibility[6] of the way unto life indicated in Hab. 2:4 and that demanded by the law. As in verse 10, so here the utterances concerning the law are understood against the background of the later Jewish redemption and merit system. The Judaizers in the churches of Galatia used the utterances concerning the law in the same context of meaning. That there is also a life in the law lived out of the *grace* of God's covenant (Psalm 119) is, of course, not denied by this.[7] Hence there is no conflict between Hab. 2 and Lev. 18 either, so long as the root of life is sought in the grace of God and thus in faith. If, however, one wants to live out of the works of the law, it is the utterances of the law itself that prove the impossibility of it.

13 Now Christ's work of redemption is suddenly brought to the fore as the one possibility of salvation. For the question might arise how then the blessing promised to Abraham, and in him to all nations, can be obtained if the law brings curse upon all who do not fulfill it. For, surely, even faith itself cannot lift the curse of the law. That is why the name of *Christ* is set in the foreground so emphatically now. In this name lies the secret of the whole redemption, that of the Jews as well as that of the

---

[6] ὁ δὲ νόμος οὐκ ἔστιν ἐκ πίστεως: the law does not lean on faith, does not find its strength in faith as a way of redemption. For Paul, faith is not a *nova lex*, a new stipulation for man to fulfill, by means of which to earn privilege with God: it is precisely the letting go of every human pretension as a ground for salvation.

[7] In Lev. 18 also such a life out of grace in the law is spoken of. Paul is not denying this. He wishes merely to point out that the Jewish scheme of redemption cannot be combined with faith. So construed, we must not blur the clarity of Paul's predications. He is not saying merely that the law in itself does not suffice, that divine help is necessary to fulfill it, and only then may we depend upon the works of the law (so M. J. Lagrange, *Epitre aux Galates*, p. 68 ff.). Rather, Paul is speaking here of the law as a *life-principle*. As such it stands diametrically opposed to faith.

Gentiles, both of whom the apostle comprises in his *us*[8] (*cf.* verse 14). Paul calls this redemption a being *purchased free from the curse of the law*. The thought of the price that had to be paid for it must not be pushed too far into the background[9] (*cf.* 1 Cor. 6:20, 7:23, and Rev. 5:9). We must think of this passage in relation to what is said in other places of Scripture about ransoming (Matt. 20:28 and 1 Tim. 2:6) and redeeming ("purchasing free": Titus 2:14). A more particular thought[10] is attached to this redeeming than simply that of the emancipation of a prisoner. At issue here is satisfaction of violated justice, as is evident from the phrase: *from the*

---

[8] Some (Zahn, *e.g., op. cit.*, p. 157) think that this can be said only of the Jews, inasmuch as these only can be supposed to live under the law (*cf.*, however, Rom. 2:14, 15).

[9] This happens when we take the sense of purchased freedom in the general sense of redemption; then we regard the question of to whom the price had to be paid as irrelevant. Then we are likely to think that Christ was the Redeemer, not because by His death He set others free from a particular penalty, but because his death was the culmination of a life in which he set men free from the thought that God deals with man on a juridical "legalistic basis" (*cf.* Burton, *op. cit.*, p. 168 ff.). Such is, however, an unjustifiable modernization of Paul's thought (*cf.* the text of the Exposition).

[10] Deismann, in his *Licht vom Osten*,[4] (1926) p. 271 ff., seeks to connect this with the so-called sacral emancipation of slaves such as used to take place in pagan temples. The practice was that when someone wished to purchase the freedom of a slave, or a slave purchased his own freedom, the sum of money involved was sometimes brought to the temple, where the priests, then, in the name of the deity, bought the slave from his master. Thus the ransoming took on a certain sacral force, although the purchase by the deity was really a fiction (*cf.* Buechsel, TWNT, I, p. 125 ff., under ἀγοράζω). As we see it such an association of ideas is not applicable here. No mention is made of a temple, a priest, of a God, but only of Christ who by His own death purchases the freedom of His own. And the price is a price not paid by God, but to God. Moreover, what is involved is not an emancipation from slavery or from prison but a payment for forfeited life, redemption from sentence of death (see text of Exposition). Finally, Paul's thoughts are not moving in the sphere of the Hellenistic religions (witness the many citations of the context), but in that of the Old Testament order of law.

curse of the law. Behind the imagery employed, there very probably lies the old practice,[11] circumscribed by the Jewish legal code, according to which ransom money could be paid for a forfeited life (*cf.* Ex. 21:30). According to this line of thought those who were under the curse were to be regarded not merely as prisoners but as persons appointed to die (*cf.* Deut. 27:15 ff. and 30:15, 19). It is from this sentence of death that Christ has redeemed them by[12] Himself "becoming a curse" for them — that is to say, a cursed one. This refers to the way in which He gave Himself to death. What we have here, in other words, as is evident also from the phrase "for us,"[13] is the thought of *substitution.* The curse, to which Christ yielded Himself victim, is not an independently operative principle, but the personal judgment of God, in which He had Christ undergo the sentence instead of the condemned ones (*cf.* Rom. 8:3 and 2 Cor. 5:21). How Christ ransomed his own in this way is not more specifically set forth. The thought is that God in His grace made the punishment accomplished in Christ valid for His own, and so brought reconciliation through Christ's death. Such a redemption (ransoming, redeeming) has not, therefore, the character of a transaction, a nice balance of the active and passive, but is a mystery of salvation in which is manifested the integrity of God's justice and His grace, and the deep bonds of unity between Christ and His own.

That Christ indeed became a curse Paul infers from the Scripture of Deut. 21:23.[14] It has rightly been observed that the reference to hanging here is not to death on the cross, something unknown to ancient Israel. The

---

[11] See, *e.g.,* G. Dalman, *Jesus Jeschua,* 1929, p. 110.

[12] The word γενόμενος makes for a temporal connection not merely, but for a causal one also.

[13] ὑπὲρ ἡμῶν: In the papyri, too, ὑπέρ is used in a substitutionary meaning (*e.g.,* in signatures instead of an illiterate person: ἔγραψα ὑπὲρ αὐτοῦ ἀγραμμάτου).

[14] Instead of "Cursed is every one . . ." both the Hebrew and LXX have "An accursed of God is . . ."

reference is rather to the hanging of executed persons on the tree of shame. Such a hanged dead person was then called "God's accursed." It is this that the apostle is applying to Christ. After His death, too, Christ hung on the cross as a condemned and executed criminal. Thus He bore the same shame as every executed criminal, and was publicly exhibited as an accursed of God. From all this it should be apparent how little justice modern theological thought does to Paul's presentation of these matters, when, for example, it talks of a God who does not deal with people on "a basis of legalism" and of a Christ who has set people free from the "fiction" of a curse of God. The reference to Deut. 21 is intended precisely to point out the reality of the curse and, in connection with it, to set forth Christ's redemption as a satisfaction of the justice of God.

14 In this verse, the apostle returns to the point of departure of his argument: the gift of the Holy Spirit, accruing also to the Gentiles, as a product of the blessing given to Abraham. All this has become possible in Christ, through His self-surrender. In two final clauses Paul sums this up as the conclusion of what has gone before. The second "that" is to be regarded as coordinate with the first. The second clause in another way says the same thing as the first clause. "The promise of the Spirit" is metonymy for *the promised Spirit* (*cf.* Luke 24:49, Acts 1:4; 26:6, and Heb. 9:15). The gift of the Spirit is now designated as the content of the promise to Abraham. It is the guarantee or pledge of the perfected redemption which Abraham was promised. And all *through faith,* that is, by way of a believing appropriation of the preaching (*cf.* verse 2), and quite without merit of works. At bottom faith, too, is fruit of the work of the Spirit (*cf.* Eph. 2:1, 5, 8 and Col. 2:13). At the same time this faith is the means by which, and the way in which, God grants the gifts of the Spirit to the redeemed by Christ.

THE LAW AND THE PROMISE

3:15-22

15 Brethren, I speak after the manner of men: Though it be but a man's covenant, yet when it hath been confirmed, no one maketh it void, or addeth thereto.

16 Now to Abraham were the promises spoken, and to his seed. He saith not, And to seeds, as of many; but as of one, And to thy seed, which is Christ.

17 Now this I say: A covenant confirmed beforehand by God, the law, which came four hundred and thirty years after, doth not disannul, so as to make the promise of none effect.

18 For if the inheritance is of the law, it is no more of promise: but God hath granted it to Abraham by promise.

19 What then is the law? It was added because of transgressions, till the seed should come to whom the promise hath been made; *and it was* ordained through angels by the hand of a mediator.

20 Now a mediator is not *a mediator* of one; but God is one.

21 Is the law then against the promises of God? God forbid: for if there had been a law given which could make alive, verily righteousness would have been of the law.

22 But the scripture shut up all things under sin, that the promise by faith in Jesus Christ might be given to them that believe.

The apostle proceeds now to look at the matter from yet another point of view, namely, from that of the history of salvation. The main content of these verses is that God first gave his promise to Abraham and that only much later was the law given out on Sinai. Hence no one may make the fulfillment of the promise dependent upon the keeping of the law. That would be to do violence to the unconditional character of the promise, and would be like modifying covenants, something which even among people is regarded as unauthorized and impossible. This raises the question of what the purpose of the law is and what its relation to the promise.

15 The vocative, *brethren,* loosens the tenseness of the tone somewhat: reproach and reprimand give way to an appeal for cordial acquiescence, something to which, indeed, the preceding verses have already formed a transition. The words *I speak after the manner of men* are not intended *in malem partem* (*cf.* 1:11) but in a general sense: I borrow a figure from human relationships. If in those relationships a settlement agreed upon, a covenant made, or a testament put in force cannot be modified, the same holds *a fortiori*[1] for what has been guaranteed to man by God.

The word that is translated *covenant* in our version originally meant an arrangement, a settlement drawn up and legally in force.[2] At least that is what it meant in

---

[1] This follows from the word ὁμῶς: literally, *in the same way.* Here it is used with adversative force: *even.*

[2] In LXX διαθήκη is regularly used as the translation of the covenant of God (*berith*), rather than the apparently more available word συνθήκη. In this there is already an expression of the fact that the covenant of God does not have the character of a contract between two parties, but rather that of a one-sided grant. This corresponds with the covenant-idea in the Old Testament, in which *berith,* even in human relations, sometimes refers to a one-party guarantee which a more favored person gives a less favored one (*cf.* Josh. 9:6, 15, 1 Sam. 11:1, Ezek. 17:13). And it is most peculiarly true of the divine covenantal deed that it is a one-party guarantee. It comes not from man at all, but from God alone. This does not rule out the fact, of course, that it involves religious and ethical obligation, namely that of faith and obedience (Gen. 17:9-10), and that thus the reciprocal element is taken up in the covenant. Still, such an obligation is not always named, and there is no room to speak at all of a correlation, in the sense that each determines and holds in balance the terms of the other, between the promise of God and the human appropriation of it. It is not the idea of parity, or even that of reciprocity, but that of validity which determines the essence of the covenant-idea. God's covenant with Noah, for

general linguistic practice. Later it came to mean a last disposition of the will, a testament. It can be taken in this last sense here also — for human arrangements are being referred to. The word *confirmed* is in the Greek[3] also derived from legal terminology. It designates a legal sanction. Paul says of such a human settlement that

example, lays down no stipulations, and it has the character of a one-party guarantee. It does of course require the faith of man, but is in its fulfillment in no respect dependent on the faith, and it is validly in force for all coming generations, believing and unbelieving (*cf.* Gen. 9:9). And in the making of the covenant with Abraham, too, in Gen. 15, the fulfillment of the law is in symbolical form made to depend wholly upon the divine deed. Abraham is deliberately excluded — he is the astonished spectator (*cf.* Gen. 15:12, 17). True, in the Sinaitic covenant, the stipulations which God lays down for His people sometimes take the form of actual conditions, so that the realization of the promise is conditioned by them (*cf.* Lev. 26:15 ff. and Deut. 31:20), but this structural change in the covenant-revelation can be explained in connection with the wider promulgation — it is to extend to the whole nation of Israel — of the covenant, by means of which the covenant-relationship takes on a wider and more external meaning. It comprises not merely the unconditional guarantee of God to those who walk in the faith and obedience of their father Abraham: it also lays down a special bond constituted by the offer of salvation, on the one side, and by responsibility, on the other side, for those who will not appear to manifest a oneness with their spiritual ancestor. Meanwhile, of course, the fact remains that in all the different dispensations of the covenant of grace, God's unconditional promise to Abraham constitutes its heart and kernel. Consequently, when the "new covenant" (Jer. 31:33) is announced, one thing is expressly made clear: namely, that the disposition which is indispensable for the human reception of the covenant-benefits will itself be granted as the gift of God Himself. In other words, that very thing which in the Sinaitic covenant was so plainly set down as a condition, belongs in the new covenant to the benefits promised by God in the covenant itself. The New Testament concept of διαθήκη lies quite in the line of that development, particularly as Paul thinks of it, as is evident in the next following chapter also, and in such a place as Rom. 9. That New Testament concept points to a salvation whose benefits are guaranteed by God and as a matter of fact are actually given, because *in* Christ and *through* Him the conditions of the covenant are fulfilled.

---

[3] κεκυρωμένην

when once it has become legal, *no man maketh it void, or addeth thereto.* Paul wants to establish this point with a view to the significance of the law in relation to the fulfillment of the promise. [The law, he says in effect, is not a later addition to the promise, by means of which the latter is robbed of its effect or subjected to new conditions. Such a thing would not be possible or warranted even among people.]

16 The first part of verse 16 constitutes the basis for the application of the figure used in verse 15. It makes the general particular, that is to say, the attention is shifted from a covenant in general to a covenant made by God, and more specifically, to His promises made to Abraham. The word *promises* supplants what is called *covenant* in verses 15 and 17. The word is appropriate because the content of God's covenant with Abraham consists of promises of salvation (*cf.* Eph. 2:12). Before the apostle goes on to shed light on the binding character of these promises, he first, by way of parenthesis, makes very clear who were the recipients of these promises, so as to remove all doubt about that, and so to define more specifically the inviolability of the promises. He takes this means to show that, in accordance with verse 7, the promises right from the start were intended for and directed to those who are in Christ or of Him (verses 28 and 29). Thus the apostle indicates the ground on which the inviolable and unconditional character of the promise rests; and at the same time he thus makes it clear again over against his opponents that the sphere within which God's promise to Abraham is influential does not coincide with that of the fleshly Israel. Concerning this last, Paul appeals to the singular of: *and to thy seed.* From this he infers that God, when He gave His promise to Abraham and His seed did not intend all of his descendants, but *the* descendant, *the* seed, who is Christ, and in Him — as appears from the later verse 29 — all who are included in Him, namely, the believers. Now it is true that many regard this appeal to the singular noun as rather remarkable. For the word translated *seed* in our version has a collective significance, also in the Hebrew and the Greek (*cf.* Rom. 4:13, 18 and Gal. 3:29), and it might be supposed, therefore, that this ground alone hardly suffices to prove that but *one* descendant or *one* portion of the seed of Abraham was intended. Moreover, it is held that the word translated *seeds* cannot in either the Hebrew or the Greek be used to refer to descendants. Many are consequently inclined to regard this whole argument about the singular noun to be simply a piece of "rabbinical invention," which does not rest on tenable ground.

There is an answer to this counter-argument, however. From the very beginning, that is, when God spoke to Abraham, a distinction was made between seed and seed. In fact, before the birth of Isaac, God had told Abraham that not in Ishmael but in Isaac should his seed be valid. This could serve, therefore, to teach Abraham how he had to regard the seed of the promise (*cf.* Gen. 17:19-21, 21:12). And this consideration could also give Paul occasion to explain that the concept *seed* is not to be taken as an indiscriminate quantity but as a unit (concentrated in the person of Christ). Objectively, therefore, the basis of Paul's distinction between the one and the many is contained in God's address to Abraham. And it is, what with the use that Paul makes elsewhere of this datum (*cf.* Rom. 9:7), very probable that this constituted the occasion for his pointing to the use of the singular, applied as it is to the person of Christ. If, consequently, we can say that Paul's exegesis of *seed* has its substantial basis in the differentiation between Isaac and Ishmael, issuing in Christ — that is in the history of the covenant in the promise — still, this does not deny that, *linguistically*, he finds the expression of it in the singular of the noun. And it may be true that this singular, taken by itself, need not designate a *single* person, and that the bearing of the passages concerning it in Genesis also is not restricted to one person. But this need not keep us from seeing in the singular *seed* an indication of Abraham's descendants concentrated in one definite person. For, from the vantage point of the fulfillment we take this seed to be Christ, and it is from that vantage point also that Paul is looking. The word used here can in both the Hebrew[4] and the Greek[5] be used to designate *one* definite descendant. That Paul is thinking inclusively, not exclusively, is clear enough from what follows. Just as in Genesis 21:12 the person of Isaac is designated by the word *seed* in distinction from that of Ishmael, though not, of course, by exclusion of Isaac's descendants, so, according to Paul, the singular of the noun is also a designation of the one Christ in distinction from all other indiscriminate descendants of Abraham together, but not in exclusion of those who are bound with Christ by faith (*cf.* verses 26-29).

17 *Now this I say*: so Paul comes to his real purpose. He proceeds to apply the figure of verse 15 to the covenant of God, concerning which in verse 16 he has first paused to indicate for whom the covenant was valid. The conclusion is *a fortiori*: the thing that holds for human agreements, namely, that they cannot be made void by

---

[4] Similarly the word זֶרַע in Gen. 4:25 and 1 Sam. 1:11 does not refer to a collective unit but to an individual descendant. For the use of the plural of זֶרַע to designate "descendants" one can appeal only to a post-Biblical period (*cf.* Gesenius-Buhl, *Hebraeisches und Aramaeisches Handwoerterbuch,* under the word in question.

[5] σπέρματα in the sense of "descendants" is used not only in the classical literature but also in the LXX (Dan. 11:31, 4 Macc. 18:1), whereas σπέρμα in the sense of a "single descendant" occurs, among other places, in Gen. 4:25, 21:13, 1 Sam. 1:11, 2 Sam. 7:12, and 1 Chron. 17:11.

addenda, holds so much more for a guarantee[6] given by
God Himself, definitively, and in full form. That raises
the subject of the law again. [For it is the law which the
heretical minds Paul is opposing in this letter are putting
into competition with the promise — at bottom, in fact,
they are placing it above the promise, for they make obedience to the law the condition for obtaining the salvation
granted by the promise. It is by this opposition, this contrast, that the character of Paul's conception of the covenant and the promise, yes, and of the law also, is entirely
governed and determined. Law means demand, conditions; the promise, on the contrary, means free grant,
guarantee, unconditionality. Those for whom the promise is intended receive the salvation. Those who do not
receive it do not belong to the seed to whom the promises
were spoken (cf. verse 16, Rom. 9:6-8). Of course, this
does not mean, as some have argued, that Paul thinks of
the law as an independent power, antagonistic even to God,
and so falls into an antinomy. For God Himself is the
author of the law (verse 19). [And the law has also a
divinely intended purpose in the history of salvation.] But
what Paul is talking about is the inheritance of salvation.
[The law cannot contribute to that.] Nor can the law, in
competition with the promise, subtract from it either.
True, the promise can also come in a form which carries
demands with it and then the pronouncement of the law
ushers in a new dispensation of the covenant of God with
Abraham.[7] But, however closely the law is bound up with
the promise in the Sinaitic covenant, the fulfillment of the

---

[6] The διαθήκην is used without the article. The emphasis is on
the qualitative character of the covenant, its divine dispensation.
The covenant is not a proposition or offer. Hence, although it is
the object of the verb, the word stands first in the clause. The
perfect participle προκεκυρωμένην as well as the emphatic ὑπὸ τοῦ
Θεοῦ serve to emphasize the absoluteness and inevitability of this
διαθήκη.

[7] Compare the exposition of verse 10.

promise is not dependent upon a human fulfillment of the law as attendant condition. Then God's covenant would no longer be a covenant (*diathêkê·*), and the promises of God would be dependent upon human factors.

The time-designation, *which came four hundred and thirty years after,* serves to make the unreasonableness of this conception plainer still. During all those centuries God's promise to Abraham had been effective without benefit of the law. How could that which came centuries later deprive the word that God had given Abraham of its power? Just how Paul arrives at the exact figure of four hundred and thirty, as the period intervening between the promise and the law, is not entirely clear.[8] For the purposes of his argument, however, less depends upon the accuracy than upon the magnitude of the figure.

18 The fact that the law cannot change or subtract anything from the divine promise has an objective as well as a temporal reason. Promise and law, as mediatorial ways of salvation, cannot be combined. If[9] the fulfillment of the law[10] must add something to the achievement of salvation, then the promise as promise, that is, as unconditional grant of God's salvation, is no longer the source and supporting reason[11] of the promised good. This

---

[8] The number 430 is also mentioned in Ex. 12:40. According to the Hebrew text of Ex. 12 these 430 years comprise the period Israel was in Egypt. On that basis, the period between the promise to Abraham and the giving of the law should be reckoned a longer period. At other places the period of Israel's oppression in Egypt is designated as four hundred years (Gen. 15:13 and Acts 7:6). The LXX transmits Ex. 12:40 in such a way that the time in which Israel was in Egypt and in Canaan came to 435 years. There is, however, no equivalent for the words καὶ ἐν γῇ Χανάαν in the Hebrew text. It is therefore impossible for us to determine whether and in what sense Paul takes his figure from one or another of these data.

[9] εἰ γάρ: the argument is purely hypothetical.

[10] The νόμου and ἐπαγγελίας are not accompanied by the article. The concern is with the qualitative aspect both in the law and in the promise.

[11] ἐκ is used here to designate the cause, the reason for existence.

promised good is now called *the inheritance* in order to qualify the certainty and legitimacy of the future blessedness.

That the hypothesis of verse 18a is unsound is stated in so many words at the conclusion of the sentence. The phrase *to Abraham* is strongly emphasized.[12] Whatever views one may hold concerning the way of salvation, the fact is that God dispensed[13] His salvation to Abraham by way of the promise.[14] And that certainly is the establishment of the covenant and the revelation of the promise to which everything else goes back. And that is the thing that must determine all legitimate instruction as to how the inheritance is received.

19 Now the question naturally arises, What is the significance of the law then in God's economy of salvation? If it cannot serve to make salvation available, what[15] end does it serve? The answer is stated thus: *It was added because of transgressions.* What now does the *because of*[16] mean in this statement? In the Greek these words can point to cause as well as purpose. If it were the former, we should have to exegete: because[17] the transgressions were many, the law was given — that is, to restrain them. From Rom. 4:15 and 5:20 it becomes apparent, however, that Paul means something else: the law was given, so to speak, to call forth the transgressions,

---

[12] In the Greek text these words stand at the emphatic beginning of the clause.

[13] χαρίζομαι without the object is a technical term from the law of inheritance: make a grant, deed something by will.

[14] δι' ἐπαγγελίας: the subject now is the means by which, the way along which, God caused His gift to come to Abraham. It is only the divine act of believing by which man can come into possession of the divine inheritance.

[15] The τί inquires not so much as to the nature of the law as to its purpose.

[16] χάριν plus the genitive.

[17] Compare for this meaning of χάριν, *e.g.,* Luke 7:47 and 1 John 3:12.

and make them manifest. This is to say more than that by means of the law sin should be *acknowledged* as transgression in its proper and terrible character: it is to say also that by means of the law sin should come out into the open and multiply itself. The law makes guilt and evil greater (Rom. 5:20).[18] This had to take place so that the indispensability of Christ would come to be rightly understood (*cf.* verse 24). Hence the sequel in this connection: *till the seed should come.* That seed was Christ (verse 16). It was He to whom the promise pointed and in whom it was materialized.[19] But, up to His coming, the law had to bring sin out more and more, and, by reason of human wickedness, call it into existence. Only in that way would the necessity of Christ's coming and work be properly understood. In contrast to what the Judaizers were teaching, therefore, the law was insufficient for salvation not only, but something which should be separated from it as far as possible.

Paul goes on to say concerning the law that *it was ordained through angels by the hand of a mediator.* From this the lesser glory of the law compared with the promise becomes manifest. The law, unlike the promise, had not come directly from God to the people, but by way of angels, and even these again proclaimed it through the

---

[18] νόμος δὲ παρεισῆλθεν ἵνα πλεονάσῃ τὸ παράπτωμα.

[19] ᾧ ἐπήγγελται: to whom the promise was come. This limits not only the fulfillment, but also the recipient of the promise, to Christ (and His own). Elsewhere, *e.g.,* in Heb. 4:1, 10:26-39, and Acts 2:39, the circle to whom the promise is directed is wider in scope. This does not make for contradiction. For the giving of the law takes place in the wider circle, without immediately introducing a differentiation into that circle. But the promise proves not to be intended for each and all; it goes into fulfillment only in Christ and in His own. It is this smaller circle to which Paul is limiting the covenant-group and the recipients of the promise. He is here speaking of the covenant, the promise, and the recipients of the promise in the narrower sense of the word.

service²⁰ of a human mediator, namely, Moses.²¹ That
the angels were of service at the giving of the law is not
apparent from Exodus. It may be that the later tradition,
which is the one being interpreted here, even as in Acts
7:38, 53 and Hebrews 2:2, takes its point of departure
from Deut. 33:2, although it is not certain that this passage refers to the giving of the law. According to some
commentators, Paul speaks of angels here because he did
not think of the law as a work of God but as a counter-
enterprise set up by angels against the promise of God.
This notion is to be rejected in consideration of Paul's attitude towards the Old Testament in general and the giving
of the law in particular (cf., e.g., Rom. 9:4, 2:18, 7:12,
and 8:7). Paul is not setting up a front against the law
as such, whose holiness and divine origin he roundly acknowledges. [But he sees in the way in which the law was
communicated a further confirmation of the fact that salvation comes not by way of the law but by that of the
promises. The law is most certainly of God, but the power
to keep it was not given along with it. God has man trans-
mit the law. But He does not Himself come with the law
in order to effect obedience to it. That is left to man.
That is why the law cannot redeem man.]

20 It is said, by way of echoing verse 17, that there
are four hundred and thirty interpretations of verse 20!
In any event, the purpose of the statement is to make clear
the significance of a *mediator* such as is mentioned in verse
19. The question is not one of the role of Moses merely,
but of the significance of a mediator generally. Into this
framework, and by way of contrast, the direct appearance
of God is mentioned at the conclusion. Everything de-

---

²⁰ We need not take the ἐν χειρί in the literal sense. It can, and
it probably does, mean: through the service of.

²¹ διατάσσειν, translated *to ordain* in our version, is a technical
term for the carrying out of laws and ordinances.

pends upon what the apostle means by *not . . . of one.*[22]
In the main, as we see it, we can choose between two interpretations: (1) Wherever a mediator is involved, two parties are involved: a mediator does not represent one party; (2) A mediator never represents *one* person merely, but comes in the name of a party of persons, a party consisting of more than one person. God, however, is one. Hence the law which was implemented by way of a mediator, does not come — at least not directly — from God, but from the many angels.

As we see it, there is no room for the latter interpretation. For one thing, a mediator need not always be delegated by more than one person. And, in the second place, this notion does not do justice to Paul's acknowledgment of the divine origin of the law (*cf.* the Exposition of verse 19). Accordingly, we choose the first explanation. The intention then is to put the emphasis on the one-sided character of the promise. The law came through mediatorial channels. Two parties were involved in it. To achieve its purpose, the law is dependent upon human appropriation and agreement. God is the author of the law, but man is the subject of its fulfillment. Hence, in the execution and maintenance of the law, all sorts of intervening persons are required. In the giving of the promise, however, no mediator intervened. God was at work alone: for He is not only the author of the promise; He fulfills it also. So it is that this mode of implementation also makes manifest the unconditional character of the promise, and its superiority to the law.

21 What has gone before might prompt the idea that there is a conflict[23] between the law and the promise, that is to say, that the law might tend to make the fulfillment of the promises[24] useless. Paul rejects this argument

---

[22] ἑνὸς οὐκ ἔστιν.

[23] κατά with the genitive means *against, in conflict with.*

[24] The form is plural: the promises made on various occasions.

forthwith.[25] The situation is actually such that the law would be the only means of justifying man, to make him guiltless before God, and grant him salvation, if only it were not dependent upon man and stopped by his obstinacy. But the law can do nothing about this obstinacy. It cannot *make* man *alive,* cannot arouse him from his impotence and grant him the ability to do what it demands. If there were such a[26] law, no other way of salvation would have to be opened up. In short, the law aims at nothing more than what the promise grants. But it cannot get man to fulfill itself. The law is not a quickening power, as is the promise (*cf.* Rom. 9:9). The promise, on the contrary, is not word, merely, but also deed, power, Spirit (*cf.* 4:21-31). And the law is without power, because of sin (*cf.* Rom. 8:3).[27]

22 The example presented in verse 21 is contrary to fact: the law cannot give righteousness. Hence it is that Scripture,[28] that is, the divine sanction and threat against the transgressors of the law contained in Scripture, *shut up all things under sin.* That is to say that Scripture has left open no avenue of escape within the pale of the law,

---

[25] μὴ γένοιτο: Far be it!

[26] νόμος: without the article, meaning *a law,* whichever it be, but from God, naturally.

[27] This interpretation of the *make alive* is more acceptable than the one which makes this word refer solely to the final end of the law — eternal life. According to the latter view the first and second clauses would mean about the same thing, and the second clause would simply be announcing a fact, without explaining it. According to our interpretation, however, the first clause explains why it is that the law cannot effect justification. And this agrees with what Paul says elsewhere in much the same sense (*cf.* Rom. 8:2, 2 Cor. 3:6, 17).

[28] In the writings of Paul, the ἡ γραφή usually refers to a specific passage of Scripture. Hence some wish to interpret this as a reference to Deut. 27:26 (*cf.* verse 10). Still, this time the expression, precisely because it does not refer to a specific passage, has a larger significance in this context. The meaning of *shut up all things* can be taken, however, as referring to such a passage as Deut. 27:26.

but has brought together as in a prison-house all[29] human life and all efforts to fight itself free. In that prison,[30] sin by its power[31] and curse makes it impossible to share in salvation. Thus God has made the law serviceable to His purpose: the law dams up and closes off all escapes to life. By the way of the law, therefore, the impotence of man to achieve his salvation has become manifest.

In the way of the divine grace, however, the purpose of all this is not negative, but positive: the intent is that all will seek escape in the way of the promise. The *promise*, that is the guarantee of salvation, which comprises the promised good within itself. The words *by faith in Jesus Christ* define this promise still further. The content of the promise flows out of the faith in Christ. Faith constitutes the connection with the source out of which issues the gift of salvation. That source is Christ. All emphasis falls on that. He gives what the law cannot give. The stress here is not so much on the channel (of the faith) along which it all issues as on the source out of which[32] it comes: namely, Christ. The concluding words: *to them that believe* after what precedes seem superfluous, pleonastic. This time, however, not merely the source of the salvation, but those who receive it also are pointed out. They are the believers, and there is no more specific delineation of them. It is clear: no new condition is being laid down here, no neo-nomism is being taught. Belief is opposed to works, as the principle of grace is to merit. This, therefore is the full-fledged break-through of the nomistic scheme of redemption.

---

[29] τὰ πάντα has in view the people who transgress the law — in their whole way of life, that is, and despite all their efforts to escape.
[30] συγκλείω is a technical term for *locking up, keeping in detention* (however, compare also Luke 5:6).
[31] In other words, sin is the jail-keeper.
[32] Hence the words ἐκ πίστεως.

BONDAGE AND FREEDOM

3:23-29

23 But before faith came, we were kept in ward under the law, shut up unto the faith which should afterwards be revealed.

24 So that the law became our tutor *to bring us* unto Christ, that we might be justified by faith.

25 But now that faith is come, we are no longer under a tutor.

26 For ye are all sons of God, through faith, in Christ Jesus.

27 For as many of you as were baptized into Christ did put on Christ.

28 There can be neither Jew nor Greek, there can be neither bond nor free, there can be no male and female; for ye all are one *man* in Christ Jesus.

29 And if ye are Christ's, then are ye Abraham's seed, heirs according to promise.

In this section the subject is no longer the difference between promise and law as means of salvation, but, quite in harmony with verse 22, the subject now becomes the bondage brought on by the law, in contrast to the redemption and freedom brought in Christ.

23 The image of being shut up in consequence of the law (verse 22) is further sustained and developed. This bondage obtained *before faith came,* that is, before the salvation given in Christ was revealed as the object of faith.[1] Instead of sin, as in verse 22, the law is now rep-

---

[1] The πίστιν is therefore to be taken as *fides qua creditur* but always in connection with the object of faith.

143

resented as the jail-keeper.[2] In other words, a kind of
modification enters into the handling of the figure of
speech, but the thought remains essentially the same.
That, after all, is why sin is so terrible and fatal for man:
it gets its power from the law (1 Cor. 15:56, Rom. 7:13,
and 4:15). Thus the apostle characterizes the state of
things before the coming of Christ. In doing so, he puts
himself in the position of those who in the way of the
works of the law try to earn their justification before God.
Paul does not here mention the fact that under the old
dispensation the law also functioned differently, not in
the sphere of merit, merely, but also in that of grace (Ex.
20:2, Psalm 119 *passim*). Concerning this positive significance of the law, Paul speaks elsewhere in this letter
(*cf.* 5:14 and the Exposition). At the moment, however,
the subject is bondage, the prison which the law brought
into being before the grace in Christ had appeared. The
character of this bondage, as will appear from what follows later, is both juridical and ethical. For, on the one
hand, the law brought wrath and curse by reason of transgression (*cf.* verse 13); on the other hand, the law, by
reason of its impotence, its inability to "make alive," was
also the means of making man conscious of his ethical
inadequacy. Its function was, by means of commands
and prescriptions, to bring him to despair, and to cause the
desire to be born in him that he fulfill the will of God in
freedom. Such a desire was in very fact also *the purpose*
of this bondage. We can deduce as much from the word
unto,[3] which has not merely a temporal but also a purposive
significance. The bondage under the law urged and forced

---

[2] Besides the συγκλείω of verse 22, φρουρέω is now also used. It
has the force of *to guard,* not merely with an eye to protection (1
Peter 1:15) but also to escape (2 Cor. 11:32). Here it is apparently
used to designate a sort of pre-arrest, which has a temporary though
probably a lengthy (*cf.* the imperfect tense) character.

[3] εἰς

man towards the faith. The apostle speaks in the first person plural, even though he is speaking not only for the Jews, but also for the more numerous Gentile readers (*cf.* 4:9). For the Gentiles, too, though outside the pale of the revelation to Israel, were co-subject to the law with the Jews, and were not without knowledge of it (Rom. 2:14-16).

That upon which all this converged is described as *the faith, which should afterwards be revealed.* In its object, Christ, and in its operation also, this faith God had kept in readiness[4] without revealing it. At the coming of Christ it had been literally *discovered.*[5] In its negative, service-eliciting character the law was oriented to and directed towards the Christ. That was its meaning and its function.

24 Once more the figure of the bondage returns in a somewhat modified form. The law is compared with a tutor, that is, with an attendant upon minor boys. The question in this connection is to what extent a positive significance should be attached to this implied pedagogy: in other words, how the *unto Christ* must be understood. Did the law (by its prescriptions for offerings, priests, purifications, and the like) consciously lead to Christ, and was it in that sense engaged in preparatory and pedogogical service, or was it so strict a master that it only did negative, preparatory work: that is, merely fostered the desire to escape from its tyranny? As we see it, the question is not whether these ceremonial regulations were also harbingers of the Christ (*cf.* the Epistle to the Hebrews), but whether Paul at the moment is concerned with that

---

[4] τὴν μέλλουσαν points not merely to the future in an exclusively temporal sense, but also to something intended for revelation and held in readiness over against that time.

[5] The ἀποκαλυφθῆναι puts the emphasis on the undiscovered character of this before the revelation; φανερόω puts it on the revelation after the concealment.

aspect of the matter. It seems doubtful. The tutor designated in the passage was not a teacher but a governor of
boys during the period of their immaturity. Slaves were
sometimes used for this purpose, men who were good for
nothing else, hard and severe to their pupils. Their name,
consequently, had a stigma attached to it.[6] And the whole
context points up the truth of being under the yoke (cf.
verses 22, 25, and 4:1 ff.). Presumably, then, we are to
understand this living under the law as under a pedagogue
or tutor, not as a gradually formative education in freedom in the positive sense, but as a growing passion for
freedom because of the oppressive yoke. The law makes
man unsatisfied, teaches him how he will *not* get to the
redemption of life. In this sense the law drives to Christ,
in order that we should be justified in Him through faith
— justified, that is, emancipated from the curse and the
impotence wrought by the law.

25-26 The statement made in verse 25 requires no
further comment after what has been said in the preceding
verse. From the function which verses 23 and 24 assign
to the law, it follows that after Christ's coming the law
as tutor, that is as seen from the vantage point of the history of salvation, has lost its significance. In that sense
it can be said elsewhere that Christ is the end of the law
(Rom. 10:4). That is not to say that the law has now
served its purpose in every respect. We must constantly
keep the theme of the letter in mind.

Verse 26 retains the figure of speech, and tells us of the
nature of the change that has taken place. Over against
the immature life of slavery under a tutor the life of sonship, with all its privileges and rights, and so the life of

---

[6] For references in this sense to classic texts, see Oepke, *op. cit.*,
p. 67.

freedom through faith[7] in Christ[8] is postulated (*cf.* 4:1 ff). In what follows later the meaning of this sonship is further delineated (*cf.* 4:5 ff.). A special emphasis falls on the word (ye are) *all* (sons of God). By this is designated, as the following verses also make clearer, the equal worth and oneness in Christ of all sorts of people. The thrust is not quantitative (head for head) but qualitative (irrespective of descent, status, race). For the way, the means, by which to arrive at this sonship is solely and simply faith.

27 Verse 27 gives us a further motivation for verse 26 which is twofold in character. First, the *ye all* is explained. All have been baptized in Christ. For by the words *as many of you as were baptized* the whole church is meant. The expression *as many* seems to limit the *ye all* of verse 26. The intention, however, is to show that in baptism lies the evidence that all sorts of people (*cf.* verse 28), without any discrimination, share in the grace of Christ. Just as little as baptism discriminates between Jews and Greeks and the like, so little can the sonship be limited to that of the natural children of Abraham. And this is what is proved by the meaning of baptism (and in this respect verse 26 is a second time motivated by verse 27) that to be baptized means: *to put on Christ.*

This close relationship which baptism establishes between Christ and the believers is also designated by the expression: baptized *into Christ*. The expression is not

---

[7] διὰ τῆς πίστεως: see the Exposition of verse 14.

[8] The words ἐν Χριστῷ Ἰησοῦ can be thought of in connection with πίστεως, or be regarded as an independent adverbial element. Most interpreters choose for the former view because the combination of πίστις (πιστεύω) with ἐν can rarely be accepted with certainty in the New Testament. If we regard the *in Christ Jesus* as an appositive to the whole (so the translation being followed), then we are dealing here with the formulation so frequent in Paul's writings, by which the oneness of Christ and His own is indicated (*cf., e.g.,* E. P. Groenewald, KOINΩNIA *Gemeenschap by Paulus,* Diss., Vrije Universiteit of Amsterdam, 1932, p. 166 ff.).

to be construed as mystical so much as corporative or federal. The baptized person is added to Christ as His own, is reckoned to His account, shares in His benefits. And the closeness of the relationship is confirmed by the exegetical expression: *to put on Christ.* Just as a garment which one puts on (or has put on: the passive translation, too, has some proponents) quite envelopes the person wearing it, and identifies his appearance and his life, so the person baptized in Christ is quite entirely taken up in Christ and in the salvation brought by Him.[9] That still leaves the question how the apostle establishes this relationship between being baptized and putting on Christ. We are not to take this in a magical or automatic sense. Baptism, too, is not in that sense an independent moment in the economy of salvation, as though oneness with Christ should take place for the believers only at baptism. Elsewhere Paul speaks of this oneness as the fruit solely of faith, without mention of baptism (*cf.* 2:19 ff.). What happens at baptism is a confirmation and sealing, a visible manifestation of what is given to the church by faith. So much is true, however, that Paul wants to indicate by his objective-sacramental mode of expression, and by appealing especially to baptism for establishing the sonship of the believers, that the reality of becoming one with Christ is nowhere so clearly revealed or so firmly founded in the Christian consciousness of faith, as precisely in this baptism (*cf.* Rom. 6:3 ff. and Col. 2:12 ff.).

28 Now the *ye all* of verse 26 and the *as many of you* of verse 27 are more particularly explained. In Christ[10] there is no descent, rank, or sex. The first contrast which Paul sets up, *there can be neither Jew nor Greek,* is to be

---

[9] *To put on Christ* becomes the equivalent of λαμβάνειν πνεῦμα υἱοθεσίας (Rom. 8: 14-17) and of "putting on the new man" (Col. 3:10, Eph. 4:24) upon whom is transferred what Christ has received (*cf.* Groenewald, *op. cit.,* p. 173).

[10] οὐκ ἔνι (an intensified ἐν) equals οὐκ ἔνεστι.

taken in a religious rather than a national sense. The gulf between these two was regarded as being so fixed and wide, not because the Gentile belonged to another nationality, but because he was uncircumcised and therefore was not an heir of Abraham. Now Paul says that this gulf does not exist in Christ but has been bridged in him. He is the seed of Abraham, and faith alone is necessary to share in the benefits of that seed.

Two further sets of contrasts are added to this one, both of them referring to the tremendous separation which social inequality and the differentiation of sexes brought with them in ancient times. True, it is the religious contrast that is the bone of contention between Paul and his opponents, but the oneness of master and slave, too, and the oneness of man and woman, in Christ, illustrates how completely the bond with Christ conquers all things and establishes them, also the removal of the first opposition (*cf.* 6:15, 1 Cor. 12:13, Col. 3:11). This is not to maintain that the natural and social distinction is in no respect relevant any more (*cf., e.g.,* Eph. 6:5, 1 Tim. 6:1, Titus 2:9, 1 Peter 2:18, 1 Cor. 11:3 ff., 14:34 ff., and 1 Tim. 2:11 ff.). From the point of view of redemption in Christ, however, and of the gifts of the Spirit granted by Him, there is no preference of Jew to Greek, master to slave, man to woman. This has social consequences, too, although the apostle does not enter further upon them at this point.

The final clause speaks positively and very emphatically of the oneness of all in Christ.[11] And it is in this way that the sense of the first clause becomes entirely clear.[12] Only the person who knows who Christ is, what He has done and is still doing, can understand how and in what sense those oppositions are obliterated. *Ye are all one*: that predication stands without the addition of "body" or

---

[11] P⁴⁶ ℵ * A have only ἐστε Χριστοῦ: presumably in connection with verse 29.

[12] Hence γάρ.

"temple" at this point. The point at the moment is the idea of oneness.

29 This verse draws the conclusion[13] and calls the attention back to the beginning of the argument where Paul called the believers the seed of Abraham (verses 7-9) to whom the promises were spoken (verse 16). Now he can postulate this with even more force, now that he has spoken of being one with, and belonging to, Christ[14] of *all* believers. If so, they also belong to the seed of Abraham, and consequently are heirs according to the promise. According to the promise: that is, according to the nature of it, not by works of the law, but by the gracious and effectual word of God. *Heirs,* originally thought of in connection with the right to the land of Canaan given to the seed of Abraham, and now comprehensive of the history of salvation in general. With this last link in the chain, it becomes clear in what sense Christ could be called the seed of Abraham (verse 16): in a corporative sense, that is, as Head of the body and of the new covenant. Always and again this one thing is reconfirmed: that belonging to the seed of Abraham is not determined by physical descent, but by faith. Essentially, in principle, the seed of Abraham is spiritual seed. If on the one hand this represents a limitation of the concept, on the other it represents a tremendous broadening of it. It is this broadening of the concept of Abraham's seed that is the subject in this context.

---

[13] The words εἰ δέ serve not to introduce sheer hypothesis, but serve to suggest the certainty of what follows: *siquidem.*

[14] There is no essential difference between Χριστοῦ and ἐν Χριστῷ It suggests still more clearly that the believers are the possession of Christ, are reckoned to His account.

CHAPTER IV

SLAVES AND SONS

4:1-7

1 But I say that so long as the heir is a child, he differeth nothing from a bondservant though he is lord of all;

2 but is under guardians and stewards until the day appointed of the father.

3 So we also, when we were children, were held in bondage under the rudiments of the world:

4 but when the fulness of the time came, God sent forth his son, born of a woman, born under the law,

5 that he might redeem them that were under the law, that we might receive the adoption of sons.

6 And because ye are sons, God sent forth the Spirit of his Son into our hearts, crying, Abba, Father.

7 So that thou art no longer a bondservant, but a son; and if a son, then an heir through God.

Once again the apostle, by making use of a figure of speech, sets forth the great change that has taken place with the coming of Christ over against being subject to the law. In these verses, too, the great theme of the letter continues.

1-2 The point of connection with the preceding context is the word *heir*. Paul had called those who are in Christ *heirs* in 3:29. This concept gives him the opportunity once more to make the distinction between the *before* and the *after*. Consequently, the present freedom of believers is not in conflict with the former service. That can happen for an *heir*. For everything depends upon whether he has already come into his rights. The question at issue in this connection, in which the figure of the pedagogue is still shining through, is whether or not he has arrived at his majority.[1] So long as he is a minor, *he differeth nothing from a bondservant,* so far at least as his having a voice is concerned. The comparison with a bondservant is made here because of the former subservience of those who now believe in Christ (verses 3 and 5, and 3:23 ff.). Although destined for freedom in Christ, they were before His coming made entirely subject to the law. Still such a minor heir is *lord of all,* that is, by right. The figure is presumably that of a son whose father has died at an early age. By the *guardians*[2] and *stewards*[3] those are meant who supervise the minor, and guard his possessions. But such guardianship and stewardship is in force[4] only until the period stipulated by the father has elapsed. To this thought the apostle will return in verse 4, when he speaks of *the fulness of the time.*

3 In this verse various features of the figure of speech are carried over. Here, too, the apostle speaks of Jews and Gentiles in a comprehensive sense (*cf.* the Exposition of 3:13), this time not as both being subject to the law but to the *rudiments* (or *elements*) *of the world.* The

---

[1] νήπιος: in this context, *under age.*

[2] ἐπίτροπος: a more general term; someone to whom the whole care of the under-aged boy is entrusted: *guardian.*

[3] οἰκονόμος: the one who has the financial responsibility, often a slave (*cf.* Luke 12:42, 16:1, and Rom. 16:23).

[4] The words translated *heir, guardians, stewards,* and *child* in our version have sometimes been construed as technical terms in a particular litigation, and an effort has been made to identify them more specifically as such. It seems more probable, however, that the apostle is accommodating himself at this point to a generally current usage, and is not thinking of a special (Jewish, Hellenistic, Roman, or even Celtic) legal procedure. In any event, in Roman law the age of majority and of entering upon his privileges as of an heir was not left to the father to determine.

meaning of this much-discussed passage is not clear.[5] As we see it, the passage has reference to definite principles or axioms (*cf*. Heb. 5:12), according to which men lived before Christ, without finding redemption in them. *The*

---

[5] στοιχεῖον (derived from στοῖχος: *layer*, or *row*) : that which has its position in a series or row, such as letters of the alphabet, or figures in a column. Hence: the elementary; plural: the elements, or *principia*. Most of the newer commentators take this consequently as referring to the elements of the heavens, the stars, which, according to the pagan-mythological conception were inhabited by demons or spirits. The star-forces or powers are then interpreted as the tyrants of mankind in the period of its minority before the coming of Christ. Paul is then representing Jewry, in its bondage to the law, as co-subject to these spiritual forces. Others put a good deal of emphasis on the fact that according to Jewish thought the angels were the mediators of the law. These are, accordingly, being represented — the argument is — as στοιχεῖα τοῦ κόσμου who stood behind the law and behind all extra-Christian worship of God. Such arguments, however, rest on very uncertain ground. For one thing, the expression which Paul uses here can be found nowhere else. One cannot speak of an established linguistic practice. Next, it is very doubtful that the spirits associated with the στοιχεῖα (in the sense of heavenly bodies) are themselves also called στοιχεῖα. But there are serious objections, too, to the material argument. How can Paul conceivably characterize, not only the life of the Gentiles, but also his own former life as a Jew under the law, as a life lived under the aegis of star-spirits? For, whenever in paganism these spirits are spoken of, the subject in question is not the maintenance of the moral law. True, Paul speaks of a connection between the angels and the law (*cf*. 3:19). But, according to the Jewish representation of this thing, the angels are not powers who tyrannize men, but rather as those who add even greater lustre to the law. That Paul had a very different personal conception of this matter cannot be proved. Hence, it seems to us quite unacceptable to suppose that Paul should in this context (4:9) speak of the angels as of *the weak and beggarly rudiments*. True, in the connection in which that expression occurs in Col. 2 there is reference also to enemy "principalities and powers," (verse 15) and of a "worshipping of the angels" which Paul must counteract. But we cannot deduce from this that the στοιχεῖα in verses 8 and 20 also refers to angels. Rather, it would seem that the expression of Col. 2:8 is being used synonymously with "the tradition of men," an objective and abstract, rather than a personal and concrete matter (See also, my contribution to the volume *Arcana Revelata*, pp. 92-94, and the literature named there).

world has not the meaning of the original creation (as those suppose who think of the "elements" as pertinent to the "law of Paradise"), but of the world in its lost estate and need of redemption (*cf.* Col. 2:8). Presumably these principles or axioms comprise what men thought they possessed in the way of potentials for redemption outside of Christ. And since the apostle speaks of being *held in bondage under these rudiments,* we shall probably have to think of the prescriptions and ordinances to which religious man outside of Christ surrendered himself, and by means of which he tried to achieve redemption. Before the coming of Christ the whole world was slavishly subjected to these *rudiments* or *elements,* also those who by means of the works of the law tried to earn their justification before God. For, even though the law itself was of divine origin, the use that men made of it was wrong. Those who lived under the law in this unwarranted way lived in the same condition of bondage[6] as that under which the Gentiles, for all their exertion, also pined.

4-5 The fourth verse speaks of the end of the period of bondage designated in the foregoing. This period of time is now spoken of as *the fulness of the time,* that is to say, the moment in which the previously determined time-limit (*cf.* verse 2) was reached.[7] Beneath this thought lies the assumption that the time[8] runs out according to a fixed plan, that time, in short, is governed. We can ask

---

[6] ἡμέθα δεδουλωμένοι: the periphrastic and the perfect participle suggest a continuing condition: we had become slaves in the most complete sense of the word.

[7] According to some, the πλήρωμα is used here in the active sense: "that, which fills" (so Burton). Generally, however, it has a passive sense: that which has been completed, the fulfilled. This passive meaning suits the context well. The picture is that of a vessel that is being poured full and at a given moment is brimful. The pleroma is not merely that last bit that fills the vessel but the whole brimful content of the container.

[8] χρόνος points to a longer duration of time (*cf.* Rev. 10:6); καιρός points to a definitely limited moment of time.

ourselves to what extent we are also to think in this connection of a process of development taking place in time, in preparation for what would happen in the fulness of time. Now it is true that God controls time, and determines the moment of the pleroma. And this carries with it the implication that the moment of the pleroma was the most suitable for what was now about to happen. But no emphasis is put upon this aspect of the matter. Nor can we prove on convincing grounds why this time was the most suitable for the coming of Christ. In any event, these words lend no support for the view that the development of time should be able to explain the advent of the Son. This advent does not have its motif in what works and ferments in time. It has its motif in what God disposes and does — though this does not at all exclude the possibility of a preparation in time. When this moment, determined by the counsel of God had come, God sent His Son. The word translated *sent forth*[9] comprises two thoughts: the going forth of the Son from a place at which He was before; and His being invested with divine authority. By this the profound and glorious significance of Christ's coming in the world is indicated. He was the Son of the Father, who stood by His Father's side already before the sending (*cf.* 1 Cor. 8:6, 2 Cor. 8:9, Phil. 2:6, and Col. 1:15). The Sonship designates not merely an official but also an ontological relationship (*cf.* Phil. 2:6). The words, *born of a woman*, do not refer to the beginning of his existence as Son, but as the child of a woman. The expression serves to suggest the weak, the human, the condescending. The woman was not only the medium of His coming into the flesh, but from her He took all that belongs to the human.[10] She was in the full sense His mother. That Paul in these words is also reflecting on the virgin birth is, as we see it, highly doubtful.

---

[9] ἐξαποστέλλω.
[10] Hence ἐκ, not διά.

For, as is evident from the absence of the article in the Greek, Paul is not putting the emphasis on His being born of Mary. Besides, the expression elsewhere is used to designate the human and nothing besides (*cf.* Job 14:1 and Matt. 11:11).[11]

The words, *born under the law,* in this context, where the law and its significance is the subject, are of special importance. By His birth from a woman, the Son also took the yoke of the law upon Himself. He took it upon Himself not only at the time of the circumcision or of His education: His birth, too, immediately placed Him under the law. The importance Paul attaches to this fact becomes evident from the following words: *that he might redeem* . . . The thought is formulated more generally here than in 3:13, where the subject was the redemption *from the curse of the law.* And, although this is certainly also intended here, still in this context the being-under-the-law is the constant bone of contention. It is this which makes man a minor without rights, a slave. Undoubtedly this is so because the law brings sinful man no redemption but only curse. The curse expresses itself also in ethical impotence or inability (see Exposition above). Christ however subjected Himself to the law in order to redeem those enslaved by it: He removed the curse for them and made them ethically free. Paul has not only the Jews in mind, but also the Gentiles. They too, though in a different way from the Jews, are subject to the law.

The second *that* gives a more specific delineation of what constitutes the redemption: the receiving of *the adoption of sons.* By this, according to verses 1 and 3, is meant sons who reached majority. Instead of the slavish yoke of the law, which set itself up between God and man, and cut off man's approach to God, Christ has wrought and has given the freedom contained in Sonship (*cf.* verse 6).

[11] For relevant rabbinical literature, see Strack-Billerbeck, *op, cit.,* III, p. 570.

6 Now the apostle returns to the thought he had recalled earlier (3:2 ff.), namely, that the Galatians have received the Holy Spirit. This is fruit and evidence of the truth that God has received them as sons. The Holy Spirit is here named *the Spirit of His Son.* This form is used, presumably, because the subject at the moment is the sonship of believers (*cf.*, however, 2 Cor. 3:17). The operation of the Spirit is characterized by this that He brings the believers to the Father, and grants them the assurance of kinship, just as the Son Himself lives in unbroken communion with the Father. Hence at one time the sonship of the believers may be called the ground for the receiving of the Spirit; at another, the gift of the Spirit may be designated as the means through which the believers become conscious of their kinship (*cf.* Rom. 8:15). In this there is no contradiction but the evidence of the reciprocity of the gift of the Spirit and sonship. Further, the reference to the sending of the Spirit here is not merely a reference to Pentecost, but to the share that every believer has in the operation of the Spirit, thanks to divine initiative. Some think that Paul has particularly the institution of baptism in mind. We cannot say, however, that Paul identifies the moment of receiving the Spirit with the time of baptism.

Concerning the Spirit, we read further that God has sent Him *into our*[12] *hearts.* In distinction from the law, which is solely an external authority and cannot change the heart, the Spirit, as the gift of the New Testament, penetrates the hearts in order to quicken and renew them (*cf.* 3:21 and 2 Cor. 3:6, 17). This is the Spirit who is *crying Abba, Father.* This cry points to the passionate, violent operation of the Spirit. At this point, the cry presumably refers to the joy of the redemption. The Spirit

---

[12] ἡμῶν, not ὑμῶν, despite the harmonizing textual variants. This change of person means nothing more than that Paul is constantly reintroducing himself into the import of the argument.

Himself is the subject of this crying. It is He who together with the believers, and in the believers, cries out to God (compare Rom. 8:26-27), and teaches them to cry out. So far as the double *Abba, Father* goes, we are not to think of an ecstatic chant in which unarticulated and unintelligible speech is used. A more plausible view is to regard the use of the Aramaic word as an expression of the deepest and most original experience of faith on the part of the apostle and the primitive Christian church — a word which, in a letter to non-Jews naturally called up the Greek equivalent. Without doubt this *Abba* also goes back to the exordium of the Christian prayer, the "Our Father." The Spirit teaches the believers to understand and pray the prayer which Jesus taught His disciples in all its comprehensive, redemptive bearing.

7 From the receiving and the operation of the Spirit, it becomes apparent[13] that the believer[14] is no longer a slave but has become a son. After verse 6 this seems to be arguing in a circle. That only seems so, however. For one thing, verse 7 is the summary not merely of verse 6 but also of all that has gone before. We have in short arrived at one of the great themes of the letter. And further, so far as the connection between verses 6 and 7 is concerned: the Sonship is not the result of the operation of the Spirit, but is rather its basis. In that sense the *because* of verse 6 designates the cause or ground. At the same time, the operation of the Spirit is evidence of sonship; it is the basis of knowledge of the Sonship, even as the latter is the basis of the existence of the former (*cf.* on vs. 6).

The conclusion is that the believer as son is also heir. This is a return to the subject of verse 1 (3:29, 18). The argument is still concerned to prove that the inheritance

---

[13] ὥστε

[14] This time, it is the singular εἶ, very personal and individuating. It applies to each separately.

guaranteed to Abraham is also intended for the believers from the Gentiles, though solely through God's gracious disposal and the divine purpose unto salvation.[15]

---

[15] διὰ Θεοῦ: this is an unexpected reading, and is therefore to be maintained over against other textual evidences. The διά points to God as Author; usually it refers to Christ as Mediator (*cf.* 1 Cor. 8:6). Hence the many corrections.

WHY FALL BACK NOW?

4:8-11

8 Howbeit at that time, not knowing God, ye were in bondage to them that by nature are no gods:

9 but now that ye have come to know God, or rather to be known by God, how turn ye back again to the weak and beggarly rudiments, whereunto ye desire to be in bondage over again?

10 Ye observe days, and months, and seasons, and years.

11 I am afraid of you, lest by any means I have bestowed labor upon you in vain.

Now the apostle returns to that point of departure which constitutes the occasion of the whole letter, and on the basis of which he, in 3:1, called the Galatians back so sharply to their duty: their return to the works of the law. After having, on all sorts of grounds, rejected this course of action (3:1 and 4:7), and after having established the sonship and the freedom of all who believe in Christ, he can now make the application in full force.

8-9 In verse 8 two sets of contrasts are in play. Formerly the Galatians were in a state of bondage. In a sense this could be understood:[1] they did not know God. *Now* they may rejoice in freedom. If they do not do so — well, that cannot be understood. For they have now come to the knowledge of God.

What the Gentiles in their unconverted condition[2] knew about God (Rom. 1:19-21) was not the true knowledge

---

[1] οὐκ εἰδότες is not merely temporal, but causal also.

[2] The ignorance discussed here does not merely designate a continuing condition, but consists also in a total estrangement from God — a separation, that is, involving the whole of human existence, and not the intellect only.

of God that is possible only through faith in Christ. From this want of true knowledge issued the life of slavish fear, and a worship of *them that by nature are no gods.* The apostle calls them gods, for so they were generally referred to. But in the same breath he says that in essence, according to their real nature, they are not gods. The reference is to the idols of polytheistic paganism which the Galatians had formerly served.

Now however there is no explanation to be given of their conduct, or any justification of it. They have learned to know God, *have come to know[3] God,* that is, as He is in Christ. Better still: they have been known by God. The bond uniting them with God was not established by them but by God Himself. He had wanted to know them as His own, interested Himself in their behalf, had chosen them.[4] There lay the real secret of the change. And the inexplicable thing now is that they are again letting themselves be tyrannized, not under duress but by choice; in fact, they seem to be deliberately planning it. Not that this time they want to serve idols; instead they want to subject themselves to all sorts of legalistic stipulations. The common element in what they did formerly and are now doing is that they are turning to "the rudiments" (*cf.* verse 3). These are now called *weak and beggarly* because they give no firm ground and comfort. And do they now wish to serve these all over again?

10 Verse 10 tells us in what this service of the rudiments consists, namely, in the observation of all kinds of ceremonial regulations, most specifically the one stipulat-

---

[3] This time γνόντες, not εἰδότες, is used. It points out the beginning of the great change. Moreover, the γνόντες, like the εἰδότες, speaks of a very particular relationship, such as that which God effects (see the Exposition of the passage). This knowledge has not the quality of a mystical union in the sense of the Hellenistic cultus-mysticism, but signifies the acceptance of God's grace on the basis of what *happened* at Christ's coming.

[4] Compare Rom. 8:29, Amos 3:2, and Hos. 13:5.

ing holy seasons.⁵ Inasmuch as Paul's argument is entirely directed against Judaism,⁶ the *days* presumably refer to sabbath-days, the *months* to the days of the new moon, the *seasons* to the Jewish feasts, and the *years* to the sabbath and jubilee years. Whether the *years* were still being celebrated by the Jews in Palestine is highly uncertain. The intent of the apostle is to say that they had taken over the whole system. The summing up of them all, the cumulative heaping up, is intended to express what is quantitatively legalistic⁷ in their course of conduct. And all this they are now busy painstakingly⁸ reintroducing.

11 Paul expresses the fear⁹ that the trouble he has gone to for their sakes has been bestowed in vain. For the

---

⁵ Those who interpret στοιχεῖα as star-spirits (see the Exposition of verse 3) see a connection between the stars and the time-divisions. The planets are presumed to regulate the calendar. As we see it, this relationship is quite unfounded. There is no evidence anywhere to show that Paul traces the origin and character of the Jewish ceremonial law to the dominion of the planetary spirits.

⁶ Some have said that it is not so much Judaism as syncretism that Paul is attacking. The assumption is that the Galatians, in their appeal to the Jewish ceremonial law, which they interpreted syncretistically, were participating in the Hellenistic cultus. The days, months, and the like, are accordingly interpreted as pagan festival and religious rites (*cf.* L. Batelaan, "De strijd van Paulus tegen het syncretisme," a contribution to *Arcana Revelata,* published in honor of F. W. Grosheide, 1951, pp. 9-21). Although the observation of Jewish law must have taken place with some modifications among the Gentiles, it can hardly be assumed that the Galatian share in the pagan cultus would be interpreted as the observation of the Torah, and be interpreted and attacked as such by Paul. The Jewish religion was altogether too exclusive for that, precisely because of its regulations (*cf.* 2:15) ; and for that also Paul stood too diametrically opposed to any sharing in the pagan cultus (*cf.* 1 Cor. 10:20) to characterize it as a careful observance of the Torah.

⁷ The καί . . . καί . . . καί . . . has an almost ironical tinge.

⁸ παρατηρεῖσθαι: to regard painstakingly; also, to observe (Luke 17:20).

⁹ The ὑμᾶς following φοβοῦμαι in the sense of *I fear for you,* or, *have fears in respect of you,* is unusual. Still, that is unmistakably the meaning. The added πως implies that what the apostle fears is not yet certain, at least not in full scope and consequence.

issue is one of basic principle. It is not the observation of religious usages as such (*cf.* 1 Cor. 16:2 and Acts 20:7) that is the bone of contention, but the basis of the justification before God. The issue is: Judaism with its autosoteriological, legalistic scheme of redemption or the gospel of free grace. These two are unreconcilable. They must choose between them. Otherwise all of Paul's trouble and exertion[10] for their sakes will prove futile.

---

[10] This lies contained in κοπιᾶν.

AN URGENT APPEAL

4:12-20

12 I beseech you, brethren, become as I *am,* for I also *am
become* as ye *are.* Ye did me no wrong

13 but ye know that because of an infirmity of the flesh I
preached the gospel unto you the first time:

14 and that which was a temptation in my flesh ye despised
not, nor rejected; but ye received me as an angel of God,
even as Christ Jesus.

15 Where then is that gratulation of yourselves? for I
bear you witness, that, if possible, ye would have plucked
out your eyes and given them to me.

16 So then am I become your enemy, by telling you the
truth?

17 They zealously seek you in no good way; nay, they desire to shut you out, that ye may seek them.

18 But it is good to be zealously sought in a good matter
at all times, and not only when I am present with you.

19 My little children, of whom I am again in travail until
Christ be formed in you —

20 But I could wish to be present with you now, and to
change my tone; for I am perplexed about you.

This portion of the letter has a strongly personal quality about it. Paul is not merely contending and arguing.
He makes an appeal to the old bond between him and the
churches. He wrestles for their love and loyalty.

12 With a strong upsurge of love, the apostle be-
seeches that they become as he is. We cannot be sure just
what is meant by this. Most probably we are to think of
the freedom in which Paul stands over against the law.
The Galatians — such is his prayer — must disentangle
themselves from their bondage, and become such as he
is. This is borne in upon them by the words: *for I also*

(am become)[1] *as ye (are).* Presumably we are to take this as meaning that Paul also tore himself loose from the legalistic position and became[2] as they. He too had wished to be saved in no other way than the Gentiles, who could not appeal before God to a single work of the law. And now that the Galatians have fallen into the hands of the Judaizers, the exact opposite must take place. They must bid farewell to their proud, legalistic pretentions, and become as he.

The words *ye did me no wrong* strike us rather abruptly and as unprepared for. Paul's sequence of thoughts is marked by abruptness.[3] All of a sudden he returns to the past, and that, as the following verses indicate, to his former stay among the Galatians. At that time he had been treated so very well at their hands.[4] And in the light of that treatment, their present changed attitude is all the more painful and inexplicable.

---

[1] We must think of ἐγενόμην as following ὡς ἡμεῖς (*cf.* 1 Cor. 9:22). Others want to interpolate ἤμην, and interpret as follows: "be free as I am free, for I too was once bound as ye are." We may question, however, whether the verb can be omitted at a juncture such as this in which a condition of the past no longer exists in the present, especially since that past condition contains no motive or explanation of the present. Perhaps we can accept the view then that Paul is referring to something which he now has in common with his readers, and which ought to serve as an inspiration to them to follow his example.

[2] That under other circumstances Paul also honored the observation of the Jewish ceremonies (*cf.* 1 Cor. 9:20, Acts 16:3 and 21:26) is to be regarded as a temporary accommodation to a point of view not yet quite established, and takes nothing away from his conviction in principle (*cf.* Gal. 2:11 ff.).

[3] Some have wanted to take these words as a reaction to a claim made by the Galatians that they had done Paul no wrong. Paul is then understood as saying, "Formerly not, but now, Yes." All this is, however, too hypothetical. Such an abrupt turn in the argument as this is happens often in Paul's writings.

[4] οὐδέν με ἠδικήσατε is a kind of *litotes:* I cannot say that I had reason to complain of you.

13 Paul in this verse probes that past experience more deeply, reminds them of events they share in common. At their first meeting the apostle had not been in a prepossessing condition. He speaks of an *infirmity of the flesh* as the circumstance under which, or the cause for[5] which, the foundation preaching of the gospel had taken place among them. If we are right in concluding that Paul is addressing himself to the churches in the province of Galatia,[6] we can think of this *infirmity* as the result of what Paul had suffered from his enemies when he brought the gospel there (*cf.* Acts 14:19 ff., and 2 Tim. 3:11). If so, the infirmity refers not to a particular disease or ailment, but to an exhausted and weakened condition ow-

---

[5] The δι' ἀσθένειαν may be interpreted as simply speaking of this infirmity as an accompanying circumstance, just as elsewhere διά plus the genitive is used (*cf.* Acts 14:22). It can also be construed causally (as in the ASV). Then the infirmity or illness becomes the occasion or cause of Paul's preaching the gospel to the Galatians. He may, for example, have been prevented by it from travelling farther, or he may have taken and found refuge from it among them. We prefer the first interpretation of διά.

[6] Whether we translate the τὸ πρότερον as *the first time* or as *formerly* will be affected, of course, by just which Galatian churches we suppose are being addressed in the letter. The first translation assumes that Paul since that time had again visited the Galatians and preached to them. The second translation does not necessarily have to assume this. If we hold to *the first time*, we are adopting the South Galatian hypothesis. Before Paul wrote this letter, he had twice visited the churches in the province of Galatia (*cf.* Acts 13 ff. and Acts 16). That Paul had twice preached the gospel in the northern territory is, however, very uncertain (see the Introduction). And since, on the basis of general considerations, the translation *the first time* seems more plausible than *formerly* (in view of the fact that such a comment would be superfluous here), we can presumably with full right appeal to the evidence of this τὸ πρότερον as support for the South Galatian theory.

ing to the molestation that he had undergone.[7] This interpretation suits very well the Greek word involved (see the Introduction, IV).

14 This infirmity is further characterized by Paul as something *which was a temptation to you in my flesh* — a temptation, that is, to despise him,[8] and to pay no attention to what he had to say. Illness, physical infirmity, and adversity were regarded even by the Jews, as representing the opposition and penalty of the deity, but more so by the Gentiles (*cf.* Acts 28:4). But instead of turning aside from him, they had received him as an angel from heaven, indeed, as Christ, the Son of God Himself. So great had their respect and confidence been at that time.

15 But now the question must follow: *Where[9] then is that gratulation of yourselves?* Once they had regarded Paul's coming as a great privilege, and had considered themselves[10] favored because of it. So much was quite

---

[7] For the rest a good many hypotheses about Paul's "disease" have put in their appearance. Some have connected it with verse 15, and construed it as an affliction of the eyes. This one is quite arbitrary, inasmuch as verse 15 has nothing to do with Paul's infirmity. More widespread is the idea that Paul was an epileptic. The alleged basis for that is 2 Cor. 12:7. In the first place there is no basis in that text for diagnosing Paul's infirmity as epilepsy; and, in the second place, it is by no means certain that the affliction of Gal. 4:13 and 2 Cor. 12 is the same.

[8] ἐξουθενεῖν: to regard as good for nothing. ἐκπτύειν: literally, to spew out. According to Oepke we are to think of a "defence-rite" based on animistic assumptions, but also applied to ordinary illnesses. It can also be interpreted metaphorically. Since the ἐκπτύειν follows the ἐξουθενεῖν this seems the likeliest view.

[9] Many manuscripts have τίς instead of ποῦ, and some have ἦν following the οὖν. According to this last reading the apostle is asking: What (at the time) was your basis for being gratified? Answer: It was not a superficial one, for . . . (verse 15b). Both readings make good sense. Probably the ποῦ in this context was not always clear, and so τίς came in as a secondary and easier usage.

[10] ὑμῶν can be subjective genitive as well as objective genitive. In any event the Galatians themselves considered themselves fortunate.

apparent from the way they had treated him. Even now the apostle can say to their credit that they would have sacrificed everything for him, even the apple of their eye[11] (*cf.* Mt. 5:29 and Ps. 17:8).

16 However, this intimate relationship has now given place to another. Paul can find no other explanation[12] than that they apparently do not want to hear the truth from him anymore. Just what Paul has in mind cannot be definitely made out. It has been held that Paul is referring to a previous letter which had disconcerted the Galatians. Less hypothetical is the view that at his second visit Paul had warned the churches. In any event, he must have plainly given them his judgment, before writing this letter, of the heretical teaching that had invaded their communion (*cf.* 1:7-9). This they had not taken in a good spirit. Hence Paul asks them now whether they no longer want to hear the truth from him.

17 The clauses of this verse are intricately complex, and in part they are hard to translate. The apostle is now introducing a third party into the argument — beyond doubt, the heretical teachers. He is talking about their motives, not about their teaching. In the first place, he says that they are making a play[13] for the confidence of the Galatians and for a favorite attitude. This happens *in no good way,* that is, it is not purely motivated, not based on good intentions. The object that they very consciously[14] have in mind is *to shut out* the Galatians. They want to isolate the churches, cut them off from other influences. Presumably the first of these other influences is that of Paul and his preaching of the gospel. The zeal which they pour into this effort is, however, purely ego-

---

[11] ἐξορύξαντες ἐδώκατε: as plastic as possible.
[12] As is evident from ὥστε.
[13] ζηλοῦν: busy themselves, bring about something. The word can be used *in bonam* and *in malam partem.*
[14] θέλουσιν: a deliberate act of the will.

istical. They do so *that ye may seek them.* After a while the roles will be reversed. Once the Galatians have been estranged from Paul, they will be dependent upon the heretical teachers, and then they will have to work under those teachers as their spiritual fathers and overseers. That is their purpose. For the moment they are zealously bidding for the favorable attention of the Galatians, in order after a while to lord it over them.

18 A right understanding of verse 18 is even more difficult, and finds expression also in the uncertainty of the text.[15] The question is as to the object of *to be zealously sought,*[16] Paul or the Galatians?[17] As we see it, verse 18b is determinative of this. Verse 18a is so generally cast that it could pertain to Paul as well as to the Galatians. But 18b seems to be concerned rather more with the devotion he would like to *receive* from the Galatians in his absence than with the devotion he *offers* them in such absence. There is no doubting the latter; it is not in dispute. The sense of the whole passage is this, then, that Paul, thinking of the efforts of the heretical teachers, admits it to be a good and desirable thing to desire the favor and love of the churches. Paul wants these himself

---

[15] The ζηλοῦσθε instead of ζηλοῦσθαι in some of the manuscripts must probably be considered as an itacism. The τό preceding the ζηλοῦσθαι in other manuscripts accentuates the infinitive form and probably was introduced for that reason.

[16] What is certain, however, is that the ζηλοῦσθαι of verse 18 must be translated passively, in view of the reiterated active of verse 17, although the passive occurs very infrequently.

[17] If Paul is the object, the sense is approximately this: "It is a beautiful thing to be the object of such zeal. I once too experienced that. But then it must be expressed in the right way, and must not cease when the person is no longer present." If the Galatians are the object, the following would be the purport: "It is a beautiful thing for you to be the object of loving care and exertion, that is, if all this happens from right motivation, and does not stop as of a given moment. So I wrought for you, and not merely when I was still among you."

also, but only *in a good matter*. Nor does he want to have it when he is with them, only to be forgotten and rejected by them when he has gone away.

19 In an affecting way, the passionate love surging in the apostle as he struggles for the preservation of the church breaks through. This is evident from the vocative *my little children* as well as from the expression that he is again *in travail*[18] for them. In this Paul's passionate endeavor for the Galatians reaches out for the language of the tenderest mother's concern. If our view of the meaning of verse 18 be right, the transition from verse 18 to 19 follows easily. The longing to be again fully desired and trusted by the Galatians brings him to this new turn of the argument, in which as the climax of this whole passage all that moves Paul in his concern for the erring churches converges on one point. The expression *to be in travail* tells of the new pain and exertion which it is costing him to give birth to the Galatians[19] as his spiritual children. The words *until Christ be formed in you* sustain that basic figure of speech. The spiritual struggle of the apostle is determined by this end, and the struggle will not cease until the end has been reached. But it is a struggle aggravated by strong misgivings as to whether the end can be attained. The pain of not having arrived at this deeply desired purpose is the dominant one. This purpose, further, is not to be interpreted as a mysterious birth of Christ in the believers, but rather, in the manifestation of their lives. It is in their lives that the form of Christ must appear in the sense that the life of the believers must be ruled by Christ, quite as much in their absolute dependence upon His righteousness as in a life according to His commands.

20 In this painful situation Paul feels the need of being able to speak to the churches personally. *I could*

---

[18] ὠδίνω: to be in the pains of travail.
[19] In 1 Cor. 4:15 he speaks of his spiritual fatherhood (γεννᾶν).

wish gives expression to a wish which for the time being cannot be fulfilled. We do not know why not. Presumably the distance was too great to permit his leaving his present duties. Nonetheless, in this decisive moment, the apostle would like to be present with them. He expects more from personal contact than from written communication. Presumably, it is in this light, too, that we are to understand the phrase: *to change my tone.* Very probably we are to think of the advantages that the living voice has over the written word. The point is not that he would be less exacting, but that in a personal conference with them he could make the readers feel what it is that moves him in their regard. *For I am perplexed about you*: the force of that is that Paul no longer knows what he must do about them and think about them in view of their baffling conduct.

HAGAR AND SARAH

4:21-31

21 Tell me, ye that desire to be under the law, do ye not hear the law?

22 For it is written, that Abraham had two sons, one by the handmaid, and one by the freewoman.

23 Howbeit the *son* by the handmaid is born after the flesh; but the *son* by the freewoman *is born* through promise:

24 Which things contain an allegory: for these *women* are two covenants; one from mount Sinai, bearing children unto bondage, which is Hagar.

25 Now this Hagar is mount Sinai in Arabia and answereth to the Jerusalem that now is: for she is in bondage with her children.

26 But the Jerusalem that is above is free, which is our mother.

27 For it is written,

> Rejoice thou barren that bearest not;
> Break forth and cry, thou that travailest not:
> For more are the children of the desolate than of her that hath the husband.

28 Now we, brethren, as Isaac was, are children of the promise.

29 But as then he that was born after the flesh persecuted him *that was born* after the Spirit, so also it is now.

30 Howbeit what saith the scripture? Cast out the handmaid and her son: for the son of the handmaid shall not inherit with the son of the freewoman.

31 Wherefore, brethren, we are not children of a handmaid, but of the freewoman.

So far as the tone of the writing goes, the conclusion of Chapter 4 differs strikingly from what has gone before. The affecting and strongly personal quality of verses 12 to 20 gives way to a more objective argument. In it, Paul once more, and now for the last time, sheds light on the great theme: the law and the gospel. Some think that this scriptural evidence occurred to Paul only after he had finished the argument of Chapter 3, that it probably presupposes further a reading in the Septuagint, and that we are to think of a kind of pause in the dictation as intervening between verses 20 and 21. Such guesses are not necessary. We may suppose just as well that Paul has saved this part of his argument for purposes of climax and capstone. The profound and striking allegory in any event once more puts the whole issue at stake between him and his opponents in the light of the sacred history. And it constitutes an excellent transition to what still needs to be said in the sequel.

21 *Tell me:* the tone is still lively and penetrating, though less tender, and more commanding now. It sounds a call to responsibility. *Ye that desire to be under the law:*[1] their conduct suggests that such is their desire (*cf.* the Exposition of verse 10). The reference is to being under the law in a demanding, prescriptive sense. There is a touch of irony here. For — such is the argument — if you wish that so much, why do you not listen more attentively to what the law says? For the Torah contains much besides stipulated commands. And whoever reads the whole of the Torah will discover that its bearing is quite different from the one the Galatians are apparently at present inclined to believe.

22 Paul now begins to argue out of the Torah in the broad sense, that is, out of the whole of the five books of Moses, to which the history of the patriarchs also belongs. From it he again takes the history of Abraham as an ex-

---

[1] In the Greek the word is used without the article: the stress is on the qualitative, normative.

ample (*cf.* the Exposition of 3:6), this time, however, in terms of what is written in Gen. 16 and 21. Although Abraham had more sons (Gen. 25:1 and 2), it is clear that the two here designated are Ishmael and Isaac. In the life of these two, most particularly in their birth,[2] the apostle sees the same opposition manifesting itself as the one which obtains between those who live out of the law and those who live out of faith. After all — such is the trend of the argument — one can be a child of Abraham in more than one sense. Hence, there is basis for this allegorization in history. The household of Abraham comprised in nucleus the people of God. And its history is characteristic of, and fundamental for, the whole history of revelation.

23 Although both children were sons of Abraham, there was a big difference between them, evident in two ways. The one was a child of a bondwoman,[3] and was *born after the flesh*; the other was the child of the free-woman, and was *born through the promise*. The two contrasts are interdependent. But the manner of the begetting is the determinative thing. Ishmael was begotten according to the order, or law, of the flesh,[4] that is, according to the natural procreative process. When Hagar conceived a child by Abraham, he had not yet become an old man (*cf.* Gen. 16:2-4, 17:17, 18:11-12). Whether the expression *after the flesh* has ethical significance in the sense of living in carnal ways without acknowledgement of God's will and promise, is something which, as we see it, cannot be ascertained. The important thing is the natural character of Ishmael's birth. It stands in contrast to Isaac's

---

[2] ἔσχεν: received. The whole emphasis on the manner of the *receiving*.

[3] παιδίσκη: a young girl, and thence, as here: a slave girl.

[4] κατὰ σάρκα

birth *through the promise.* The preposition *through*[5] indicates that the promise in this instance called life into being. In verse 29 *through the promise* becomes *after the Spirit.* Thus the effectual power of the promise becomes characterized as the power of the Spirit. In this, in the power of the Holy Spirit, which makes alive and regenerates, the real secret of the covenant of the promise consists, and in that it has its reason and its fulfillment. The promise is not simply an offer made on stipulated conditions. To this contrast between what man supposes he can do in his own strength and what God alone can give, Paul's conflict with the Judaizers also goes back. It is the contrast which from the very beginning has, on the one hand, accompanied and, on the other, opposed the fulfillment of the promise from the human point of view.

By his *born through the promise,* Paul obviously assumes that God qualified Abraham and Sarah for the sexual act so that they could bring forth a child (*cf.* Heb. 11:11). We are not to think of a fatherless birth, as some Jewish theologians construe the birth of Isaac. Nor are we to think of the speculations of other Jewish teachers according to which Abraham and Sarah were sexless, and only later received the organs of procreation.

24 The allegory spoken of in this verse is not merely the product of exegesis but is plainly indicated in the history of Abraham's sons.[6] The two women named in verse 23, Hagar and Sarah, *are* (that is to say, represent) *two covenants.* The reference is to the covenant with Abraham, characterized by the promise, and the covenant of Sinai, which gets its nature from the law (see the Exposi-

---

[5] διά with the genitive. One can consider whether the article belongs in the text. It is missing in א A C P[46]. Without the article the whole emphasis falls on the qualitative aspect of the promise. When read with the article, the meaning again becomes the particular promise which God gave to Abraham.

[6] ἀλληγορέω can mean either (a) to speak in allegory, or (b) to expound in allegory. Here the first meaning is in place.

tion of 3:18). At bottom there were not two covenants, but two dispensations of one and the same covenant of grace (*cf.* Ex. 20:2). Still these two can be contrasted to each other here. For, irrespective of the fact that the covenant made at Sinai was a privilege for Israel, inasmuch as there the Lord accepted Israel as His people and they were thus established (Ex. 19:6), still the nature of this dispensation was determined by the law. And this law, however much it was the evidence of God's gracious concern for Israel, could itself bring no redemption: for sinful man, indeed, it was a yoke which he could not bear. The idea of bondage, which played so great a role in earlier verses (*cf.* 3:23 and 4:7), comes back in full force now, this time in connection with Hagar, the bondwoman. Just as she could bear Abraham only a slave-child, because in the birth of her son it was not the power of the divine promise that operated, but that of natural procreation, so the law, for as long as it was oriented to human strength — and so it was among the Jews — could only foster the spirit of subservience, the mentality of a slave (*cf.* Rom. 8:15). Hence it can be said of the covenant that is from mount Sinai, characterized as it is by the mount of law-giving, that it *is Hagar.* What it brought forth was in origin and result the same that Hagar brought forth. She represented the same life-principle and life-type. Concerning the other woman, Sarah, and her significance, only verse 28 speaks.

25 The meaning of this verse in the context is far from clear. The difficulty has a relationship to the uncertainty of the text.[7] As it seems to us the attempt is a

---

[7] Two questions are involved. The first is whether or not Ἀγάρ belongs to the text. The second is whether δέ or γάρ follows the τό at the beginning of the verse. The comparative value of the several textual authorities gives no help here. In the Exposition we take account of the translated version which accepts Ἀγάρ, even though the reading without Ἀγάρ seems to us the right one. See below.

mistaken one which finds in the name *Hagar* (if this name
is, indeed, original in this context) the explanation for the
similarity posited in verse 24 between Hagar and Sinai.[8]
Rather, this verse is intended to make clear to Gentile
readers the connection between Hagar and the present-day
Jerusalem. The first part of verse 25 continues to draw
the line from Sinai to Jerusalem, and has a sort of concessive force. It is true that this Hagar represents mount
Sinai in Arabia,[9] but she is, however, to be identified with

---

[8] The big difficulty is that nobody can say how Ἁγάρ can,
linguistically considered, be a designation of Sinai. Chrysostom
says that mount Sinai, in the language of the natives, was spoken
of as Hagar. We do not know on what basis this statement of
Chrysostom rests. Others point to the Arabian *hadjar*, which means
rock or stone, and even today serves to designate particular rocks in
the Sinai range. And it is considered possible, accordingly, that
Paul, perhaps on the basis of rumors picked up during his Arabian
journey, came to think of *hadjar* as a name for Sinai. Obviously
this would be to lay down a very arbitrary relationship between
Hagar and Sinai, the more so because it should become evident
from this relationship that Sinai, like Hagar, gives birth to slave
children. And all this then would have to be ascribed to the
allegorical method. Quite rightly, Zahn writes that such a thing
might be conceivable for an Alexandrian but not for Paul. And in
the cited materials there really is no evidence for such a view at all.
And on the ground of this impossibility of finding in the name
Hagar a connection with Sinai, many suppose the Ἁγάρ is an interpolation. As we see it this conclusion has much in its favor. We
can ask, however, whether it is not possible to give another exegesis
of the text *with Hagar*. See the Exposition above.

[9] This interpretation is even more plausible if the Ἁγάρ is left
out of the text: "For (or: now) Sinai is (it is true) a mount in Arabia,
but . . ." Others, who prefer the version without Ἁγάρ, think that
in the words *for Sinai is a mountain in Arabia* there lies the
explanation of what has gone before, namely, that Sinai brings forth
children unto slavery. They point to the subjection of the tribes of
Arabia, who regard themselves as descendants from Hagar; or they
point to the location of the mountain outside the pale of the promised land, and suggest that therefore this whole Sinai-dispensation
lies outside the domain of the fulfillment. But these explanations
seem very forced. Arabia cannot simply be called a country of
slavery and bondage. And as for the location of Sinai outside the
territory of the holy land, that can hardly serve as evidence of its
inability to effect freedom. Jerusalem, in the heart of the promised

the Jerusalem so strongly propagated by the heretical teachers. The purpose of this verse, consequently, is to continue the old contrast of verse 24 and to enhance it. In present day Jerusalem that is taking place which once proceeded from Sinai: the bondage of the law. *For she is in bondage with her children.* The figure of the mother is sustained. Present day Jerusalem also propagates bondage, for it knows no other redemption than the law. The word *children* in this predication refers to fleshly Israel, seen as a single unit, and seeking its hope in the works of the law. These children are set in contrast, of course, to the free seed pre-figured in Sarah's child, concerning whom more is now to be said.

26 Over against the Jerusalem *that now is* the apostle sets the Jerusalem *that is above.* The temporal definition has its opposite in the spatial one. One might have expected that instead of *above* we would have had another temporal designation, say, *that will be.* But this other Jerusalem already *is,* though in another way than the Jerusalem of the bondage. It is *above,* that is, in heaven, and not like the earthly one to be empirically approached. By this other Jerusalem Paul means not merely the assembly of those who have left the earthly struggle to enter heaven: he means also the central point from which believers are gathered, nourished, and governed, and the manner in which all this takes place. That is *above,* for Christ is there, and there is the citizenship of believers (Phil. 3:20). It is their spiritual gathering place (Heb. 12:22). This is the *free* Jerusalem.⁷ Those who belong

---

land, could not grant freedom either. Hence, as we see it, the concessive meaning of verse 25a is greatly to be preferred. The writer is then explaining how he arrives from Hagar by way of Sinai at Jerusalem. And then it is not a matter of major importance whether we read γάρ or δέ, for the γάρ need not refer solely to the first part of the clause. If in 25a we read δέ, the word would have only a connective, and not an adversative, force.

to its community are not born for bondage, but for freedom, and are educated in it. Not the law, nor the thing they themselves must do, but grace, that which they have received in Christ, determines their life. Hence Paul can refer to this Jerusalem as to a *mother,* for those who belong to it owe their spiritual existence to it. For the gospel of Christ is a redeeming, emancipating, and quickening word of power.

27 In support of the foregoing, Paul cites Isaiah 54:1.[10] This quotation is taken from the prophecy of Zion's restoration and magnitude after the captivity. In this prophecy the promise is made that she that is barren and forsaken, like a woman separated from her husband and without children, will have more children than in the time when she, before the captivity, had not yet been forsaken by the Lord. This the apostle applies to the relation between the present Jerusalem and the heavenly one. The last is a mother by the grace of God, even as Zion was after the captivity. Her progeny does not depend upon natural development or exertion, but upon the divine miraculous power which grants life where it seemed impossible, and that in such abundance that it far surpasses the possibilities offered by the flesh. Paul sees the fulfillment of this promise in the gathering of the believers in Christ. It is a gathering made not from among the Jews only, but from among the Gentiles also. The apostle comprises in one glance the divine word of power directed to the barren Sarah, the promise to an Israel sunken away in captivity, and the preaching of the gospel both to the Jews and to the Gentiles. The common element in them all is the power of the divine word, by which they receive life, freedom, and eternal redemption. *This* is the seed of Abraham, the people of God, the true Jerusalem. This Christocentric view of history gives new insight into the

---

[10] According to the text of LXX, that is, though with only minor variants from the Hebrew.

fulfillment of prophecy. Still, all this is not merely an interpretation and a point of view over against Scripture. It is a laying bare of the true sense of the Scripture: *for it is written*, which rests on the unity of the divine work of redemption in history.

Isaiah 54:1 characterizes Zion as a barren woman. In the last two lines the figure of speech is shifted a little. The cause of the childlessness is sought for in the husband's desertion. Not all of the implications of this permit themselves to be particularly applied to the reality of the situation. The main thing is the blessing of children which comes from the miraculous power of God. The whole history of the people of God, from Abraham on, is full of that miracle. The Church is the fruit of God's regenerating grace, not of human effort. And this truth is to be developed further in the letter.

28 Now Paul makes the application to his readers. His tone is mild again, and persuasive. They who have fallen into the clutches of Judaism must understand that they are children of Abraham in the manner of Isaac. That had been the subject all along: sonship in Abraham. But the manner in which one is born to Abraham as his child, and the way in which one belongs to him, determines everything. *As Isaac was*[11] points not only to the similarity but also to the nature of the genetic bond. So much can be deduced from *the children of promise,* that is, children who owe their existence to the promise, they who were called into being by the life-giving, miraculous word of God. In Isaac this became apparent from the circumstance of birth; in believers it becomes apparent in the quickening, the regenerating, of the Spirit (*cf.* verse 29). But in both instances, God's power and sovereign grace is the cause of the birth. Hence the zeal to bring the Galatians under the law again is a profanation of the divine work, also as that work operated in history. Hence,

---

[11] κατὰ 'Ισαάκ.

too, the allegory is not arbitrary. The household of Abraham is the prototype of the church of God. The promise which accrued to him is the secret of the maintenance of the church. Ishmael's and Isaac's birth represent the two attitudes towards the promise: that of human self-vindication and that of faith.

29 The allegory is developed still further. The analogy appears not only in the way in which the two kinds of seed are born, but also in the way the one kind treats the other. In the days of Abraham, too, the fleshly seed persecuted the spiritual. The reference is to the enmity between Ishmael and Isaac (*cf.* Gen. 21:9). In this context,[12] the word *persecuted* means — as is evident from the comment *so also it is now* — not so much a threat to life as one to freedom and security. It was so that Ishmael had persecuted Isaac. He did not leave Isaac in peace, grudged him his priorities, his privileges. And it is just this that the apostle finds in the action of the Judaizers against the believers. They are not content to be different themselves, but cannot bear the others. In this that old principle manifests itself which throughout the ages has operated also among the people of God. That which is fleshly lays snares for that which is spiritual.

Very important again is the characterization of the dual conflict by means of the words *born after the flesh*[13] and *(born) after the Spirit.*[14] What in verse 23 had been

---

[12] It has been held that the incident referred to here cannot without qualification be called persecution, and that Paul is following the rabbinical *halacha*, according to which Sarah would have been aware that Ishmael as in a bit of fun bore down on Isaac with bow and arrow (*cf.* Strack-Billerbeck, *op. cit.*, III, p. 575 ff.). It is very questionable, however, whether one may use a tradition, which arose only in the post-Christian Palestinian Judaism, as an explanation. Paul's word reflects nothing of the kind. Nor can one hang such a theory on the ἐδίωκε. As is also suggested by the comparison which Paul makes (*so also it is now*), it can better be regarded in a somewhat mitigated sense.

[13] ὁ κατὰ σάρκα γεννηθείς.

[14] τὸν κατὰ πνεῦμα.

called *born through promise* and in verse 28 *children of promise* is here designated as *born after the Spirit*. For it is the Holy Spirit who makes the promise effectual. And just as this Spirit quickened life in Sarah's aged womb, so now the children of the promise are they whom the Spirit has made alive (*cf.* 3:21), regenerated, and these now manifest themselves as such.

30 Scripture teaches also however that the threats and enmity of the fleshly seed must be resisted. The apostle appeals in this connection to Sarah's words of Gen. 21:10, which, according to Gen. 21:12 are approved by the Lord, and therefore are valid as an authoritative Scriptural statement. Sarah sees in Ishmael's presence a constant threat to her son Isaac. She requests that Hagar and Ishmael be sent away, and that he be excluded from the inheritance.[15]

This passage of Scripture should serve to warn the Galatians not to let themselves succumb to the clutches of the Judaizers. Rather, they must avoid this contact with a slave-principle, and defend themselves against it. Else the inheritance may escape them.

31 The *wherefore* is not so much designed to draw a conclusion from the immediately preceding as to offer a general summary of attitude after all that has been said in verses 21 to 31. Again there is the shift to the first person: it includes Paul, the Galatians, and everyone who accepted the gospel. On this basis in the sequel the apostle will point out the obligations that issue from such acceptance.

In this separation of the two kinds of seed, a separation which cannot be obliterated, both the divine disposition and human responsibility manifest themselves. God's cove-

---

[15] οὐ μὴ κληρονομήσει: definitely a negation. Some manuscripts, instead of the future indicative have the aorist subjunctive, which would be expected after μή, and probably therefore is due to correction.

nant with Abraham, the seed of Abraham, the obtaining
of the inheritance — these are realized most deeply in the
quickening power of the promise, that is, by the Holy
Spirit. The gulf between the one seed and the other, between the children of the bondwoman and the children of
the free, depends upon the good pleasure of the divinely
initiated covenant and upon His promise. It does not depend on human accomplishment.

The promises determine the conduct of those who receive them. That is how it is, and not the other way
around, as though the promise were determined by the
conduct of those who receive it.[16] But this does not ab-
solve man of his human responsibility. Wanting to inherit
the promise in some other way than in that of faith disparages the divine work and is therefore culpable. Hence,
in the claim, *we are children of the freewoman*, there is
no ground for glorying at all. But there is in it an incentive to watchfulness not to let the received grace slip
away.

---

[16] Compare Schniewind, TWNT, II, p. 579, under ἐπαγγελία.

CHAPTER V

FOR THE LAST TIME: EVERYTHING OR NOTHING!

5:1-12

1 For freedom did Christ set us free: stand fast therefore,[1] and be not entangled again in a yoke of bondage.

2 Behold, I Paul say unto you, that, if ye receive circumcision, Christ will profit you nothing.

3 Yea, I testify again to every man that receiveth circumcision, that he is a debtor to do the whole law.

4 Ye are severed from Christ, ye who would be justified by the law; ye are fallen away from grace.

5 For we through the Spirit by faith wait for the hope of righteousness.

6 For in Christ Jesus neither circumcision availeth anything, nor uncircumcision; but faith working through love.

7 Ye were running well; who hindered you that ye should not obey the truth?

8 This persuasion *came* not of him that calleth you.

9 A little leaven leaveneth the whole lump.

10 I have confidence to youward in the Lord, that ye will be none otherwise minded: but he that troubleth you shall bear his judgment, whosoever he be.

11 But I, brethren, if I still preach circumcision, why am I still persecuted? Then hath the stumbling-block of the cross been done away.

12 I would that they that unsettle you would even go beyond circumcision.

---

[1] This translation depends upon the most important documents. Other manuscripts have ᾗ instead of τῇ; still others have τῇ ἐλευθερίᾳ ᾗ. The fact that ᾗ has not a regular recurring position in the manuscripts makes this variant less acceptable. Its insertion before ἡμᾶς may be owing to dittography. Materially, also, the rendering of the best manuscripts is very convincing. By means of asyndetic statement the apostle gives force to his expression of the principle of freedom.

The argument in this section still fits in the framework of what has gone before. It constitutes the conclusion of the preceding. It has a sharply polemical and practical quality. The more theoretical argumentation has ceased.

1 Very emphatically the freedom of the believers is placed in the foreground here as the purpose[2] of Christ's redemptive work. There is an antithetical drift in the argument, which comes to expression in a very richly pregnant, almost ironical, way. The self-evident quality of the utterance ought to make it superfluous: Christ did not set us free for slavery but for freedom! By this freedom is meant dismissal from subservience to the law (*cf*. 3:13, 22-25 and 4:1, 2, 21-31). It is a freedom from the curse of the law (3:13, 24), but also from the spiritual impotency from which the law cannot rescue man (3:21; *cf*. Rom. 8:3). Since the demand of the law continues, this spiritual inability takes on the character of a spiritual death (2 Cor. 3:6, 7). It is from this guilt-establishing and deadening power of the law that Christ has redeemed them by liberating them from the curse of the law and by raising up His own from death unto life (2 Cor. 3:6, 17). This took place — such the thrust of *Christ set us free* — through the death and resurrection of Christ which, through the power of the Spirit, also works life and freedom in believers (*cf*. 2:19, 20; 3:2; 4:6, and Rom. 7:4). And therefore the falling back into subservience is inexplicable and inexcusable.

Over against that the second clause comes with the positive: *stand fast*.[3] It is an appeal for a resolute and steadfast perseverance in freedom against every effort to bring them again under the yoke of slavery. The reference is again to the yoke of legalistic prescriptions (*cf*.

---

[2] The dative ἐλευθερίᾳ is sometimes construed as instrumental. As we see it, a dative of purpose or designation makes better sense.

[3] The στήκετε derived from στήκω has intensive effect.

verse 2). This is not to say that the law has no further use (*cf.* verse 14 and Rom. 8:4), but outside of Christ the law has no claims upon the believers any longer; so far as both its mandatory character and its content go the law must be seen and judged entirely from the point of view of Christ (*cf.* 6:2 and 1 Cor. 9:21). The word *again* points to the fact that the Gentiles, too, although the law had not been given to them as it had been given to Israel, are nevertheless co-subservient to it (*cf.* 4:3-5). *Be*[4] *not entangled* is to be taken in a reflexive sense: let themselves be kept in the yoke.

2 With the greatest possible force Paul now lets his apostolic authority come to expression: *Behold, I Paul say unto you.* He puts his readers before the dilemma: circumcision or Christ, everything or nothing. Do the false teachers want to persuade the Galatians that they must seek out the right combination of the two? Paul denies the possibility. The issue is not circumcision as such, as though circumcised persons could not be saved, but circumcision as the Judaists were demanding it of the Gentiles as a condition for obtaining salvation. The sufficiency of Christ's work is what is being challenged. True, the Galatians have not yet entirely yielded[5] to the opponents, but they are being prodded in that direction and seem turned that way (*cf.* 4:10). Hence it is necessary now to set the whole matter in sharpest focus and consistency, and to see through its implications.

3 Verse 3 gives a further explanation[6] and confirmation of verse 2. The stately emphasis of verse 2 is now continued in the words: *Yea, I testify to every man.* What

---

[4] The present tense points to a new, continuing condition which would obtain if the Galatians were to listen to the Judaizers.

[5] ἐάν plus the subjunctive gives expression to possibility.

[6] The δέ is not adversative here but conjunctive.

is said here has the power of a formal testimony[7] which has general, universal validity. In verse 2 the apostle had said that Christ is all or nothing for man. Now he applies this same exclusive principle also[8] to the law, and first of all to the law's demand. He who submits to circumcision subjects himself to the whole law, must take the whole law for his reckoning. Apparently the readers did not know this. They did not want to surrender Christianity entirely to Judaism, but lent their ear to those who taught that without circumcision one could not receive the promise made to Abraham. Paul however puts the dilemma: the one *or* the other. That at other times he did not in all instances regard circumcision as objectionable (*cf.* Acts 16:3) is not in conflict with this sharp distinction. It is not circumcision that is an impediment to Christ, but the legalistic-soteriological motive underlying it.

4 Once more, and very clearly, the thrust of verses 2 and 3 is restated. The way in which man is to be justified before God is the thing that is in question. Here, now, are two exclusive principles: Christ and the law. If the Galatians again seek to be justified[9] through[10] the law — for such is the meaning of their drift towards circumcision — they give evidence of being separated, estranged, cut loose from[11] Christ. The apostle faces them

---

[7] Compare 1 Thess. 2:12, Eph. 4:17, and Acts 20:26, 26:22.

[8] It is approximately in such a sense that we are presumably to take πάλιν. Some think that it refers to an earlier oral statement by the apostle. As we see it, we shall have to explain it within the scope of the logical argument here being conducted. Paul is now repeating in reference to the law what in verse 2 he had said in reference to Christ. Hence not *in the second place* but *again*. It may be that the absence of πάλιν in some manuscripts is owing to a failure to understand the connection.

[9] δικαιοῦσθε: *de conatu.*

[10] ἐν is instrumental.

[11] καταργοῦμαι ἀπό: to be cut off from relations with someone or something, to have nothing further to do with something (*cf.* Rom. 7:2, 6).

with this logic in order to bring them to the point of reflection (*cf.* verse 10). That is the force of *ye are fallen away*[12] *from grace.* In this, grace proves to be the life-principle, a grace wrought by Christ and received through faith.

5 Verse 5 presents the contrast[13] represented by the emphatic introductory pronoun *we.* It refers to those who together with Paul fix their hope not on the law, but on Christ. Every word of this sentence is more particularly explained in the preceding chapters and constitutes an appeal to what has been said in them. *Through the Spirit* refers to the Holy Spirit in His life-giving power, establishing the bond between Christ and His own. The phrase stands in contrast to *by the law* (verse 4), that is the law which works death and not life, slavery not freedom, despair not hope. The words *by faith* more exactly define the opposition of the two: what the Spirit gives and works is known and received by faith. This gift is further characterized as *the hope of righteousness. Hope* is objectively, not subjectively, meant: the thing hoped for, the object of the hope. This object consists of[14] *righteousness.* As is evident also from the words *we wait for,* this righteousness is designated as something of the future. The apostle has his eye on the final verdict of acquittal in the divine judgment. Elsewhere, in Rom. 5:1, for instance, he speaks of righteousness in the past time, that is, as a verdict of acquittal that the believer has already received. But here the reference is to the verdict which God will pronounce before every ear and eye. In reference to this the Judaizers are demanding circumcision. The hope spoken of in this

---

[12] ἐχπίπτω: originally used for the falling out of a flower: to be loosed from something, to lose one's grasp of.

[13] The transition is formed by γάρ, however. In other words, verse 5 gives the explanation of the loss of grace named in verse 4: salvation is possible only if we "through the Spirit . . . wait for the righteousness."

[14] δικαιοσύνης is a genitive of explication.

verse consists of a great longing and a positive certainty.[15] Judaism cannot offer this certainty and therefore does not know this hope. It can never be sure which way the scales will tip.

6 The words *in Christ* refer not so much to the person of Christ as to the economy of salvation granted in Him. And this is again set in contrast to the sphere of life in which those move who look for their hope entirely or in part to the works of the law. Verse 6 gives a more detailed confirmation and explanation of verse 5. That Paul could speak as he did in verse 5 was based on the fact that being circumcised or not[16] has no meaning for being justified — not now, after the coming of Christ. He is talking quite objectively again: the reference is to circumcision in itself, as a physical condition[17] (but see also Rom. 4:11). To this he opposes faith. Of that it can be said that it *availeth,* not because it is the fulfillment of a *nova lex,* but because it brings Christ alone into relevancy. Moreover, the apostle suggests that faith is not ethically indifferent. Hence he introduces *love* into this context, something to which he will give more attention later (*cf.* verse 13 ff.). Faith is *working through love.*[18] One may hold that the Judaizers made the charge against Paul that by

---

[15] The prepositions in ἀπ' and ἐκδεχόμεθα lend an intensifying force.

[16] All of the substantives of this passage are without the article so as to bring out the qualitative element the more strongly.

[17] περιτομή and ἀκροβυστία: *concretum pro abstracto.*

[18] The ἐνεργουμένη is certainly to be regarded as a middle. In this there lies an old controversy with Roman Catholic exegesis and dogmatics which speak of the *fides caritate formata.* This concept, according to the Aristotelian notion of form, makes love rather than faith the determinative idea. But this conception, quite apart from philosophical interpretations of ἐνεργουμένη, is indefensible on linguistic and material grounds. For one thing ἐνεργεῖσθαι is regularly in the New Testament taken in an intransitive sense (*cf.* Rom. 7:5, 2 Cor. 1:6, Eph. 3:20, 1 Thess. 2:13, and 2 Thess. 2:7). Moreover love does not precede faith, but faith precedes love. The operation of faith through love is not to be understood in a synergistic sense, as though faith through its expression of love cooperates

preaching faith he was minimizing or even neglecting love as the fulfillment of the law. In response the apostle says that faith expresses itself, so to speak, in love. The thought contains the two truths that love is fruitful (cf. James 2:22) and that the energy of the works which love produces is quite different from the "works" of the law. This energy is a working of faith which has its principle and its source in the life-giving power of the Spirit. In accordance with the promise and in communion with Christ's death and resurrection it brings into manifestation also the new life of believers.

7-8 Paul again recalls (cf. 3:2; 4:9, 14) the attention of the Galatians to the time when they had not yet under the influence of the Judaizers taken a wrong turn. He uses the figure of running in the race-course. They had gotten off to such a good start, seemed eager to bend every effort to living the life of service for Christ. Who now has hindered them from obedience to the truth?[19] The question is not prompted by ignorance, but by amazement. What kind of people were these false teachers anyhow, and what did the Galatians expect of them, to warrant such an about-face? By *the truth* the gospel is meant. The truth is not exclusively intellectual, but determines the whole of man's attitude toward life. Verse 8 speaks of this new influence in connection with the preceding as a *persuasion.*[20] It cannot be said of this persuasion that

---

in producing salvation, but is to be construed as an operation in an absolute sense. In the way of love (δι' ἀγάπης) faith reveals and proves itself. See also Oepke, *op. cit.,* p. 92.

[19] Some manuscripts add μηδενὶ πείθεσθαι after πείθεσθαι. That makes for the version: "Who has hindered you? Obey no one (i.e. be persuaded by no one) not to obey the truth." The determination of the right reading is difficult. The omission of these two words, since they make for an unusual expression, is the easier to explain; moreover, one can explain the omission as an instance of homœoteleuton. Far and away the most and the best manuscripts have the shorter version.

[20] πείθεσθαι ... πεισμονή.

it *came of him that calleth you.* The utterance is designed
to remind the readers of the time when the gospel had
brought about such a conversion. That was when they
had the experience of being spoken to by the irresistible
divine voice and been brought to obedience to the gospel.
And, of course, even now they did not mean to deny *him
that called* them. But they must nevertheless bethink
themselves that their listening to the new voice is not merely an exchange of it for the divine one: it is to become
apostate from the voice of God. The pressure being put
upon them this time comes from an entirely different
quarter from that from which they were once called.

9 Very probably this is a proverb (*cf.* Mt. 13:33)
with the meaning: small causes, big results. The fatal
element in Judaism is that by placing something alongside
of Jesus (the circumcision, for instance) it at bottom denies the work of Christ (*cf.* verse 2). At stake in this
matter is a principle. Like leaven this principle will prove
to be of very comprehensive significance.

10 Although the apostle has time and again indicated
how seriously he takes the spiritual condition of his readers (*cf.* verse 4), he now nevertheless expresses his confidence[21] that the Galatians after what he has so far written will agree with him. This confidence is based on the
communion in Christ, in which Paul knows his readers
and himself to be included, and on which he has fixed his
hope, also with an eye to his readers. From this it is
evident, too, that in verse 4 he was not yet speaking of
accomplished facts. It was the fear of such an outcome
which made him speak so absolutely as he did. For the
heretical teachers themselves, however, the apostle knows
no condonation. He speaks of them in the singular number, perhaps by way of designating the Judaists in as
general a way as possible (*whosoever he be*). It may also

---

[21] The ἐγώ gives a strongly personal quality to this statement:
"I for myself cannot think otherwise than that they . . ."

be because a particular person[22] appeared as the leader among them (however, compare verse 12). In that event the words *whosoever he be* mean: irrespective of how important and esteemed the person may be or may act. The thing that he (or they) have brought about is *trouble,* that is, spiritual unrest and confusion in the church concerning the way of salvation. This is the result of the effort to combine Christ and the works of the law. The judgment upon this will not fail to come, however, and the party which has caused the confusion will have to bear his penalty as a heavy burden. Although God's name is not mentioned, it is clear that Paul has in mind the judgment of God.

11 There is difference of opinion about the meaning of verse 11.[23] As we see it, Paul is here simply mentioning the hypothetical case that he himself, just as the

---

[22] That this is Peter (Lietzmann) or that in the end it should perhaps prove to be James (Oepke), cannot be demonstrated on the basis of anything in the letter, nor by anything we know about relationships in the early church of the New Testament.

[23] The question is what is meant by the words: *If I still preach circumcision.* Some think that Paul is here reflecting on a charge made against him, namely, that he himself in some instances clung to circumcision or even recommended it (Acts 16:3), and was therefore in a poor position to be admonishing others on this score. Others judge that Paul is not in this instance attacking the Judaizers, but is fighting on a second front against the antinomian enthusiasts, who themselves hold it against Paul that he has not quite conquered his own Judaism. But these views seem to us to have little in their favor. Concerning the last named theory, it seems right to remark that we know nothing about such a radical antinomianism in Galatia, and it would certainly not be brought into the discussion in such an unexpected and indirect a way. As for the first view — that Paul preached circumcision as a necessary condition for salvation — that could hardly be successfully charged against Paul by anyone. And even though we must reckon with the possibility that some among them blamed him for inconsistency, there is nothing to suggest that he is at the moment referring to that charge. And this takes no note of the fact, further, that such an alleged inconsistency could hardly be denominated a "preaching of the circumcision."

Judaizers supposed it mandatory, might even now, after the coming of Christ, be preaching circumcision as an indispensable condition. He would then no longer have to dread persecution, or opposition, or traps set by the Jews and by those who were letting themselves be led by the Jews. For then *the stumbling-block*[24] *of the cross* would be removed. Now the cross means such a stumbling-block, for it rejects all human merit and glory and learns to expect all good only from the crucified Man of Sorrows. This is an offense and a vexation to men (1 Cor. 1:23). And if the requirement of circumcision were maintained, the center of gravity would be returned to man.

The apostle puts forward this hypothetical case in order again to set in a clear light the consequences of what the Judaizers wanted and demanded. The case is not real: it is intended merely to show that the work of Christ, which quite entirely eliminates man, and therefore is so offensive, is the thing at issue.

12 With these last words which testify to a deep disparagement and disdain, Paul now turns aside from the heretical teachers. Once more he characterizes them as they *that unsettle you,* that is, bring you into a condition of revolt, prod you on. The word gives expression to a despicable enterprise. Now he again speaks of his opponent in the plural (*cf.* verse 10).

Paul's last word to these teachers is a malediction whose content is described in the translation *even* (to) *go beyond circumcision.* Presumably this is a reference to self-emasculation.[25] The apostle does not have in mind the self-mutilation which occurred in ancient Israel and which brought the threat of banishment from the church of the

---

[24] σκάνδαλον really is the bit of a stick which keeps the trap from falling until one touches it: hence, the occasion for falling, sinning; a stumbling-block; an offence. τοῦ σταυροῦ is a genitive of origin or is epexegetical.

[25] ἀποκόπτομαι; also in the profane literature the word sometimes has this meaning.

Old Testament (Deut. 23:1), but rather sacral castration which was practised in some pagan religions and cults.[26] If Paul wishes that the heretical teachers submit themselves also to this operation, usually undergone in a condition of raving madness, one would have to think of it in a sarcastic sense. That they should pay attention to his wish was not to be expected in any event.[27] The apostle wishes merely to say: Whoever means to do God a service and to foster holiness by the circumcision of the pagans must not do half-work. He had better follow the example of the pagan priests who in their raving antics yielded themselves to unnatural abominations. In this way Paul disqualifies the effort of the Judaizers in the severest way: he puts the circumcision of the Gentiles on the same level as the most abysmally sunken pagan superstition. This remarkable fierceness over against the circumcision can be explained out of his passionate desire to keep the gospel of Christ free from all self-engendered increments which are well calculated to denature it. Such a mutilation of the gospel stands for Paul on one and the same level as the most despicable pagan practices, by means of which men tried to assure themselves of the favor of the gods.

---

[26] In the cult of Attis, for example, whose most famous temples were at Rome and in Phrygia in Asia Minor.

[27] ὄφελον (Attic ὤφελον) plus the indicative future need not in the Koine necessarily introduce an unattainable wish. Apparently, however, it must be taken here in the sense indicated in the text above.

PART THREE

The New Life
Through the Holy Spirit
5:13-6:10

In this next main section of his letter, Paul comes to the religio-ethical application which so often constitutes the conclusion of his letters. He does this, however, in very close connection with the preceding: *negatively,* by the admonition that the freedom in Christ may not be taken as a freedom for the flesh; and, *positively,* by setting forth the service of love in its inseparable oneness with the salvation in Christ, indeed, by setting it forth as the integrating constituent element of that salvation. The ethical is not an independent thing, and does not depend upon human freedom, but is in its entirety determined by the soteriological and Christological main content of the letter.

SPIRIT AND FLESH

5:13-25

13 For ye, brethren, were called for freedom; only *use* not
your freedom for an occasion to the flesh, but through
love be servants one to another.

14 For the whole law is fulfilled in one word, *even* in this:
Thou shalt love thy neighbor as thyself.

15 But if ye bite and devour one another, take heed that
ye be not consumed one of another.

16 But I say, Walk by the Spirit, and ye shall not fulfil the
lust of the flesh.

17 For the flesh lusteth against the Spirit, and the Spirit
against the flesh; for these are contrary the one to the
other; that ye may not do the things that ye would.

18 But if ye are led by the Spirit, ye are not under the law.

19 Now the works of the flesh are manifest, which are
these: fornication, uncleanness, lasciviousness,

20 idolatry, sorcery, enmities, strife, jealousies, wraths,
factions, divisions, parties,

21 envyings, drunkenness, revellings, and such like; of
which I forewarn you, even as I did forewarn you, that
they who practise such things shall not inherit the kingdom of God.

22 But the fruit of the Spirit is love, joy, peace, long-suffering, kindness, goodness, faithfulness,

23 meekness, self-control; against such there is no law.

24 And they that are of Christ Jesus have crucified the
flesh with the passions and the lusts thereof.

25 If we live by the Spirit, by the Spirit let us also walk.

13 What with the rejection of the law as a means for
achieving righteousness before God, the Jewish fear that
the gospel of Christ might undermine the great ethical
force which, despite everything, issued from the Jewish
religion of law, is quite understandable. Understandable

also is their fear that the Christian life would not offer enough defense against the ethical normlessness of Paganism. For that reason, Paul, after he has maintained the sufficiency of the gospel of Christ over against the synergism of Judaistic Christianity, not only stresses the necessity of the ethical life, but also points out its bases and its inter-relationships.

The introduction to this is a full maintenance of the freedom wrought by Christ (see the Exposition of verse 1). The *ye* is placed at the beginning for emphasis: it marks the contrast with the bondage of the false teachers. The whole statement shows cause: over against the confusion brought about by the Judaizers (verse 12) there is the clear calling of Christ to freedom. By the divine word of power,[1] through the Holy Spirit (see above), they have been brought out of the captivity of the law (see the Exposition of verse 1) into freedom. Now follows a limitation: this freedom may not become an occasion[2] for the flesh, that is, for sinful human nature, for wicked impulse. The flesh wants freedom to express itself as it will. Christ has not called the believers for such a freedom. Hence Paul immediately lays down the requirement of *service* — that is, service for each other. Christ set them free, so that they might be able to do *that*. And the *through love* shows the way in which this service must take place.

14 It is characteristic of Paul's mode of thinking that he should return to the law at this point, and bind the command of love upon the hearts of the Galatians by an appeal to the law. The law is and remains for him also an expression of the will of God. Nevertheless, he does not bind believers to the law in the concrete and historical form of the Torah, but in the form of the command of

---

[1] καλεῖν: in the effectual sense.
[2] ἀφορμή (ἀπό and ὁρμάω): point of departure, bridgehead, occasion.

love, in which the whole law[3] has its summary and fulfillment.[4] This summary of the law, which came to expression long ago in Leviticus 19:18, is, together with the
command of love to God, taken as the epitome of the law
also in the teaching of Jesus (Mt. 22:34 ff., Luke 10:25
ff.; *cf.* Matt. 19:19 and 7:12). That Paul is referring
back to this, just as he does in Rom. 13:9, is not expressly
stated, but can definitely be accepted. Elsewhere too he
speaks of the law of Christ (6:2 and 1 Cor. 9:21). In
this entire summary, Paul's purpose is both to let the law
come into its own proper validity in the life of believers;
and to graft its fulfillment upon a different principle from
that of human self-vindication through works — namely,
the salvation brought by Christ. For the love, in which
the law has its fulfillment, is the fruit of faith (verse 6).
Thus in this Epistle the apostle can on the one hand pro-
claim freedom from the law, and on the other can require
love as the fulfillment of the law. This fulfillment remains
a divine requirement. But since the law, as demanding
agent, cannot effectuate the fulfillment, it is not the imperative of the law but the bond of faith in Christ which
forms the ground and origin of the fulfillment of the will
of God. This does not remove the requirement, but bases
it upon the salvation brought by Christ (compare verses
1, 13, 24, and 25). *Thy neighbor* means any and all whom
God puts upon our way (*cf.* Mt. 5:43 ff.). *As thyself*:
that is, as self-evidently and as intensely as thyself. Basic
to this thought is not the notion that we must love our-

---

[3] ὁ πᾶς νόμος: the law considered as a unit as distinguished from
the individual commandments.
[4] πληρόω has the force not only of the doing of the law, but also
of its interpretation (*cf.* Matt. 5:17 ff); such an interpretation, in
other words, as does full justice to its bearing and context. In connection with ἐν ἑνὶ λόγῳ which designates an activity of thought,
we shall have to conceive of πεπλήρωται in this sense: the whole
law finds in this one word its total expression (*cf.* Rom. 13:9). The
perfect tense suggests the definitive, to which one need not again
return.

selves also, but rather the thought that self-love is natural, instinctive, to man. Just as directly and unhesitatingly as he loves himself, one must love his neighbor. The fact that Paul does not speak of the love for God in this connection does not mean that he regards it as of less importance. Love for God is much more the source and the condition of love for the neighbor (Mt. 22:38, 39). What is evident from the omission is that Paul is not giving a systematic treatment of ethics here. He speaks according to the need of the moment, and has his eye on human social relationships.

15 To *bite* (wound, inflict pain) and to *devour* (leave no room for) and to *consume* constitute a climax. It is to be understood of various gradations of social hatred and jealousy. Some refer this discussion to the extant differences in the churches brought on by the work of the heretical teachers. There may be truth in this, although it is very clear that Paul does not condemn, but rather commands, a resolute attack upon those teachers. Hence, we presumably are to think of the life "after the flesh" more generally. It is the life which becomes dominant when the freedom in Christ is denied or abused. Then it goes from bad to worse. This, too, could come of it,[5] that the Galatians would drive each other wholly to spiritual destruction so that deliverance would no longer be possible.

16 Over against this giving each other and themselves up as a prey to sin, Paul, continuing in the line of verses 13 and 14, emphatically presents to his readers ("I say") the vision of the Christian life. In this *the Spirit* and *the flesh* are opposed in irreconcilable conflict. The Spirit is the worker of the new life in the fellowship of Christ's death and resurrection (*cf.* 2:20). The *Walk by the Spirit* goes to show that this life realizes itself not only in Christ but also in the present historical reality of the be-

---

[5] ἀναλωθῆτε: subjunctive aorist: things have not yet reached such a pass, but threaten to come to it.

liever. He must *walk* by the Spirit, that is, he must in fellowship with Christ let himself be ruled by the Spirit. The principle of the Spirit does not make human effort unnecessary, but arouses it and equips it to put all its forces into the service of the Spirit. The tense of *walk* points to a continuing condition. The life through the Spirit does not consist of a separable series of deeds, but assumes an inner conversion which is sustained by God (*cf.* verse 25). The second clause adds to this a statement about the future: *ye shall not fulfil.*[6] He who walks by the Spirit will be able to resist the flesh in the end — resist it, that is, in its wicked desire[7] bent on total domination.

17 The desperate necessity to choose one or the other, the Spirit or the flesh, becomes apparent from the irreconcilable conflict between them, and from the strength which the flesh too continues to exercise. The desire of the flesh takes offence at the Spirit which wants to put it in bondage. Hence, too, the Spirit is also the great enemy of the flesh, and its desires[8] are diametrically opposed to those of the flesh. This antithesis is once more expressly postulated in explanation of the opposed desires. The question is how we are to understand the last clause.[9] As we see it, the words *that ye may not do* speak of the result

---

[6] οὐ μή when taken with the subjunctive aorist or the indicative aorist is the most decisive form of denying a future event.

[7] ἐπιθυμία: originally *vox media*, the word is here modified to mean evil desire by the addition of σαρκός.

[8] Only as an exception is ἐπιθυμεῖν used for the desire of love (*cf.* Luke 22:15).

[9] One can take the ἵνα as either final or consecutive. If the former is accepted, one must ask who it is that postulates this purpose. And, presumably, one would have to think, then, of the flesh as well as of the Spirit. However, it is very difficult, logically, to regard these two opposing principles as the common subject, both together realizing this purpose. Hence we prefer the idea of a consecutive use although it is not an original use, and is limited even in the New Testament. Elsewhere, too, however, such a weakened but consecutively colored meaning can be found (*cf.* 1 John 1:19, Rev. 9:20, and Luke 9:45, and others).

of this irreconcilable conflict: because of it the believers, too, do not do what they want to do[10] by virtue of the new man in them. Thus comes the struggle between willing and doing (Rom. 7:13 ff.). This is a general truth. There is always the resistance of the flesh. Irrespective, therefore, of what the believer wants to do, this counteracting influence is always at work. Hence the new life, too, is subject to a penetrating, internal dualism. Still, this is not the last thing that can be said of the matter. It is not passivity but action that is in order. According to verse 16, believers must in this dualism conduct the fight against the flesh. That becomes apparent from verse 18.

18 Over against the not doing "the things that ye would," the apostle poses something else, namely, the being led of the Spirit.[11] The result of that will be: no longer being under the law. The *if ye are led* does not imply that believers are passive; it is at the same time a matter of letting themselves be led (*cf.* verse 16). The thing does not happen without regard to their will. In this, too, the Spirit is the principle of the new life, and by it the flesh is resisted and its conquest is impeded (verse 16). The concluding *ye are not under the law* designates the condition of curse (*cf.* 3:13), bondage (*cf.* 3: 22, 25, and 4:1-3), impotence and spiritual death (*cf.* 3:21), which has so often been described in the preceding portions. In this verse the emphasis is on the spiritual inability in which man lives, if he has only the law. He is defenceless against the flesh. In this lies the connection with the preceding verse. If one is to offer resistance in the struggle between Spirit and flesh, one must be in the service of the Spirit and not in that of the law. That the demand of the law remains (verse 14) is not denied, of course. The issue,

---

[10] The θελεῖν does not refer simply to the willing of the natural man.

[11] The εἰ is not purely hypothetical but introduces a condition of fact. The first clause is, however, the presupposition of the second.

in short, is the strength, the power, that is necessary for the fulfillment of the law.

19-21 Now the apostle proceeds to describe the desire of the flesh in its concrete expression.[12] To this he will later contrast the fruit of the Spirit. Of these works of the flesh, he says emphatically, first of all, that they are *manifest*. This does not mean to say that they always happen in public; it means rather that they can plainly be recognized as works of the flesh (*cf.* Rom. 1:19). No one need be mistaken about that.

Of the vices which Paul names here, the first are related to sexual aberrations such as often came to the fore in the paganism of that day and its cultic extravagances. But we are, presumably, also to think of the general statements which Jesus gave in the Sermon on the Mount (*cf.* Mt. 5:28 ff.). *Fornication* refers to illegitimate sexual intercourse in the widest sense of the word.[13] *Uncleanness* in Paul's writings is always used in an ethical sense, and often, as apparently here also, in the sexual sense. *Lasciviousness* means the lack of restraint, abandon.

The nature of the sins named in verses 20 and 21 is different. *Idolatry* is the service or worship of images in a pagan sense; the word occurs only in Christian literature. *Sorcery* originally means the preparation of medicines; more pregnantly it comes to mean the preparation and application of magical devices. The word, accordingly, also lies in the sphere of idol-worship and magic. *Enmities,*

---

[12] This so-called catalogue of vices shows some variations in the different manuscripts. In a few, the list begins with μοιχεία, that is, adultery. In some instances, too, the difference amounts to uncertainty about a singular or a plural. And φόνοι follows φθόνοι in some manuscripts. It is easy to understand, of course, that in such listings various changes, omissions, additions, and the like, should appear. Lists of sins, similar in kind, occur repeatedly in the letters (*cf.* Rom. 1:29 ff, 13:13, and 1 Cor. 5:10). In profane literature, too, especially the Stoical, one encounters similar catalogues.

[13] Some derive the πορνεία from πέρνημι. The meaning would then be: intercourse with a prostitute for a fee.

being plural, stresses the continuous and the numerous. *Strife, jealousies,*[14] *wraths*[15] designate the sins of a loveless, egoistic, and unrestrained social life. *Factions*[16] are intrigues, machinations, the use of objectionable methods. In the same direction are *divisions,* schisms, and *parties,*[17] that is, camps and sects. To these verse 21 adds *envyings,* that is, envy in all its manifestations, *drunkenness,* and *revellings* — drinking-bouts, carousels, and orgies. All these, and the like of them, for the list is by no means exhausive, are works of the flesh and form an impediment to coming into the Kingdom of God. To this the apostle testifies with all the authority of the ministration of the keys (*cf.* Mt. 16:19); he does so solemnly *beforehand.* He says it *now,* that is, now that he must counteract the heretical teachers who give themselves out as supporters of the law. But he has said it *before* also, in precisely the same way, when he was with them in person. For the preaching of the gospel has never meant a yielding to sin. *Who practise such things*: not sin as such so much as the obtuseness to conversion, the living in sin, prevents the entry into the kingdom of God. That kingdom is to be understood here in its eschatological significance. And there is no doubt about this judgment: *they shall*[18] *not inherit.*

22-23 In this part the fruit of the Spirit is set in contrast with the works of the flesh. The whole passage reminds one of the description of love in 1 Cor. 13:4-6.

---

[14] ζῆλος: zeal: also used *in bonam partem.*

[15] θυμός: originally the meaning was *breath,* then disposition. In the New Testament it is often used to designate an outburst of passion or wrath.

[16] ἐριθεία is often brought into context with ἔρις. It stems, however, from ἔριδος: wage worker. Thence its metaphorical sense.

[17] αἱρέσεις comes from αἱρέομαι: to choose. It refers to the choice one must make between various opinions; thence the official opinion itself, the party, the sect. Later it also means heresy, that is, a meaning distinguished from the true one.

[18] The future tense connotes certainty.

The word *fruit* indicates more plainly even than *work* that the issue in this matter is not what man himself can do. A fruit is not something that is made or done. It comes up out of a definite principle, in this instance, the principle of the Spirit. The singular stresses the fact that what the Spirit works constitutes a unity. By this fruit of *the Spirit* no particular *charismata* in the sense of 1 Cor. 12 is intended but rather that which the Spirit grants to all who live by Him. In all this, human responsibility is not, of course, eliminated. Rather, the possibility is indicated by which this responsibility can be fruitfully assumed.

Love, joy, and *peace* stand at the head of the series. As is evident from the context, love is to be understood especially as the love for the brethren (*cf.* verse 14 ff.). As the fruit of the Spirit, this love is entirely determined by the salvation granted in Christ: that is, its motive (*cf. e.g.,* Mt. 18:23 ff.), its intensity (*cf. e.g.,* Mt. 18:22 and 5:43 ff.), and its object (*cf.* Lk. 10:30 ff.). *Joy* has religious sense here: delight in God because of the salvation in Christ, the reconciliation, and being received as children. In this the gospel quality of the fruit of the Spirit is clearly evident. It comes out in *peace* also. In the New Testament, the word can in general designate a condition of blessedness and well-being that will arrive in the grand future (*cf.* Lk. 2:14); it can mean also the peace brought by Christ between God and the believers (Rom. 5:1); it can mean, further, the removal of enmity between men in their relations with each other (Eph. 2:14 ff.); and it can mean, finally, the affective state of those who trust in God (Rom. 15:13 and Phil. 4:7). In this connection, it presumably points particularly to human social relationships. In this sense, *peace* can form the transition from *joy* to *long-suffering.* The last term assumes attack, provocation, incentive to wrath. And the fruit of the Spirit makes for the preservation of love and peace despite these all. *Kindness,* which is named here as in 2 Cor. 6:6 alongside of *long-suffering,* designates the expressions which the latter takes. *Goodness* refers to an attitude towards others. Faithfulness,[19] in this instance, is to be understood in a religious sense. It can also be translated as *loyalty* (Rom. 3:3 and Tit. 2:10), and this rendering is probably the preferable one. *Meekness* is elsewhere (Mt. 5:5) designated as meekness over against God. Here the force is ethical: gentleness, tolerance. The last word of the series, *self-control,* means personal temperance in general. It can be interpreted as referring specifically to sexual relations (1 Cor. 7:9) as well as to pleasures in general, and signifies restraint, moderation. Sometimes, however, it refers to self-control in the expression of love to others.

These, then, are the gifts that the Spirit gives to those who permit themselves to be guided by Him. But it is true of such also that the law does not turn against such as they.[20] The antithesis, law-gospel, still lurks in the background. The *against* expresses the fact that the law constitutes a threat to man. It not only *subjects* man to itself, constituting him a slave, but also takes position *against* him. The reference presumably is to the curse, the spoliation, which the law brings upon the disobedient (*cf.* 3:10, 13). Hence the law is not *against* those who walk by the Spirit because in principle they are fulfilling the law (verse 14). In this again it is evident that the requirement and the strength of the law continue. But the fulfillment of the law is guaranteed now, in Christ, by the Spirit. Hence that takes place which was impossible for man and for the law, and the threat of the law is lifted.

24 The lordship of the spirit brings with it the crucifixion of the flesh. For the flesh is also present with those

---

[19] πίστις

[20] One can regard the τῶν τοιούτων as being neuter also. Even if, in view of the context, one should prefer this, he would still have to interpret it in such a way that those who live accordingly do not have the law against them.

who exhibit the fruit of the Spirit (*cf.* verse 17). If in this connection, therefore, we read of *they that are of Christ Jesus,* this is no news. For it is Christ Jesus that grants the Spirit (*cf.* 2 Cor. 3:17). Now, however, believers are named for Christ, for the apostle speaks of the *crucifying* of the flesh. Their belonging to Him (*cf.* 3:29) makes for a full life-fellowship between Christ and the believers (*cf.* 2:19 ff.). They share His cross, too, in so far as Christ there bore the curse of the law (3:13), and broke the power of sin. So the lordship of the flesh and its passions is also denied. That is part of what was overcome on the cross. Hence it can be said of those who are of Christ that *they have crucified the flesh.* There came a moment of time[21] in their lives in which they were taken up into that fellowship of life, and in which, therefore, the dominion of the flesh over them was broken. The phrase *to crucify* is intended to designate the relationship with the cross of Christ, and also to express the absolute rejection and denial of the flesh. It does not mean that since that moment the flesh can no longer bring an influence to bear, but rather that its corruptness is acknowledged and is assigned to death, not by the cross of Christ alone, but by the believers themselves also. By the *passions*[22] *and the lusts*[23] *thereof* we are to think of the sinful, corrupt urges such as have been indicated in the preceding discussion. In all this the flesh, the sinful nature, is revealed in its total power and influence.

25 It may be doubtful whether this verse is the conclusion of the preceding matter, or the introduction to the applicatory material still forthcoming in the letter. The

---

[21] Some relate this to the time when faith began, others to the time of baptism. The one need not rule out the other. Baptism *a posteriori* confirms the favor obtained by grace.

[22] πάθος: passion, that which operates in man, even though he does not will it.

[23] ἐπιθυμίαι: the desires in which the παθήματα work themselves out. But the two words are approximately synonymous here.

transition is fluid. Verse 25 picks up where verse 16 left off, and the sequel gives it a new concrete development.

The chiastic construction gives this short statement unusual force. It proceeds from a definite assumption (*If we live by the Spirit* . . .), the truth of which must prove itself (*by the Spirit let us also walk*). The first points out the principial relation to the Spirit. He is the new life-principle of freedom (*cf. 2 Cor. 3:17*). He grants the effectual power of divine grace which operates through Christ in the believers. The second clause speaks of the activity of believers which they exercise in the strength of the new principle granted them. In accordance with that they must live. The Spirit must also become the norm, the rule, of this manifestation of life.[24] He creates a new life-style. And this new manner of life must be made manifest, must be distinguishable. Paul includes himself. For the believers this walking by the Spirit remains a constantly renewed mandate and a continuous exertion.

---

[24] The στοιχεῖν is more rigid than the περιπατεῖν of verse 16. The idea of a row or rule is contained in it. It is used for movement in a definite line, as in military formations or in dancing.

CHAPTER VI

MODESTY

5:26-6:5

26 Let us not become vainglorious, provoking one another, envying one another.

1 Brethren, even if a man be overtaken in any trespass, ye who are spiritual, restore such a one in a spirit of gentleness; looking to thyself, lest thou also be tempted.

2 Bear ye one another's burdens, and so fulfil the law of Christ.

3 For if a man thinketh himself to be something when he is nothing, he deceiveth himself.

4 But let each man prove his own work, and then shall he have his glorying in regard of himself alone, and not of his neighbor.

5 For each man shall bear his own burden.

This segment enters deeply into the practice of walking by the Spirit. The emphasis is especially upon living with each other spiritually, not in haughtiness but in modesty and in the consciousness of one's own imperfection.

26 This last verse of Chapter 5 puts the social life of the believers among each other under the point of view of modesty. A person is *vainglorious* when he swaggers in vain things, when he brags. Such an attitude is provoking, challenging, precisely because the one is so eager to amount to more than the other. The other side of the same thing is envy, jealousy. The person who wants to be first cannot stand the success of another. Self-glorification goes hand in hand with jealousy and provokes it. The context does not suggest that taking pride in the works of the law is peculiarly the issue in question. But it is most particularly spiritual pride that the apostle has in mind (see the sequel).

1 As opposed to self-exaltation, the apostle, resuming an ingratiating manner, asks for gentleness and sympathy even towards those who have been caught in an act of sin. This idea, at least, seems best to give the thought of Paul's *to be overtaken in any trespass*.[1] In other words, a very serious offense is assumed. A person (a member of the church, that is) is caught hard upon the act of sin.[2] His guilt is manifest, and he stands ashamed. It is such an instance that must bring to light what walking by the Spirit is. Such is the force of *ye, who are spiritual*. This is not being said in levity, irony, or flattery; it is said to point to the criterion of being spiritual. In such an instance one may not exalt himself, but must help the sinner to leave his evil way, and to bring him back into the status of believers.[3] Presumably *the spirit of gentleness* does not refer to the Holy Spirit Himself, but a human spirit directed by Him (*cf.* 5:22). The corrective effort must be made in gentleness and friendliness. This is necessary not only with a view to the sinner who is involved, but is in agreement also with the vigilance which everyone must maintain over himself. *Looking to thyself* implies being sharply attentive, very vigilant, and continuously so. Being spiritual does not automatically protect one against sin. *Lest thou also*: what happened to the other person

---

[1] The meaning of προληφθῇ is not quite certain. Some interpret it as: to be overcome, taken unawares, by sin. Although the verb permits of this view as well as of the one expressed in the translation followed here, and although it makes for a very good sense, it would seem, in view of the following ἐν τινι παραπτώματι the least warranted of the two. These words can better be taken to refer to the place where the overtaking happened than to the means or the agent of it.

[2] παράπτωμα contains the idea of falling. It is not the deliberate, the planned, aspect of sin that is stressed here, but rather the unwitting element. Mistake rather than misdeed is the force of the word, though without absolution of responsibility.

[3] καταρτίζειν: to straighten out, to set in order.

can happen to you also. There is an active power which induces to sin, namely, temptation.[4] That man is not himself capable of protecting himself against it (Mt. 6:14) is not, of course, being denied. But this fact does not make his own watchfulness superfluous, but rather the more imperative (1 Cor. 10:12, 13).

2 The *burdens* apparently in the first place refers to whatever oppresses man spiritually, threatens to induce him to sin, or to keep him in sin. This is pictured as a burden because one goes bowed under its weight and fears that he will succumb to its pressure. In the bearing of such a burden the Galatians must help and support each other. This is to be an exercise of spiritual fellowship, designed to help them stand by each other in the struggle against sin, and in the event of defeat to raise one another up again. In doing this they will be fulfilling *the law of Christ*. Not that in such a statement Christ is being set up over against Moses as a new lawgiver. The claim of the law which was once given continues in effect (*cf.* 5:14), but this accrues to the believers from Christ. He stands between the law and believers. He guarantees its fulfillment in believers by the Holy Spirit. The new element is not the content of the law, although Christ's coming and His work modified it, but in the root of obedience, namely, Christ. And above all the bearing of another's burden harmonizes in every respect with what Christ by word and deed taught His own. In this real love becomes manifest, the fulfillment of the whole law (*cf.* 5:14).

3 The apostle continues the same theme: self-inflation[5] is also self-deceit. The words *when he is nothing* have an even more absolute force about them in the Greek. The force of them includes not merely the various faculties of

---

[4] πειράζω is used *in bonam partem* as well as *in malem partem,* that is, as *trying,* and as *tempting.* The temptation lies not only in the active influence of sin in man, but also in the circumstances which favor such an influence.

[5] δοκεῖ: subjective in sense, in this connection meaning: *to vaunt.*

man, but is more general. Seen by himself, no one amounts to anything, measured by the true, divine norm. And in the positive sense, all that anyone is he is by the grace of God. That is something which an arrogant self-inflation cannot see. Else self-esteem would not exist. Consequently, too, it exalts itself on the basis of nothing, and so its folly becomes manifest. Who then would not care to be on guard against it?

4 Again the apostle throws man back on his own self. It does not make sense to esteem one's self more highly than others. What matters is what a person is and does himself. Let him weigh his own work, that is, prove it,[6] and make his judgment on the basis of that. And the measure he must apply in making the proof is the true norm given by God Himself. To use the faults of others as a norm is to make it too easy for oneself! The possibility of glorying[7] must arise from one's own work. It might seem that this emphasis on glorying is a contradiction of what the apostle has just said in the preceding verses. We must remember, however, the most fundamental self-criticism has been enjoined upon the Galatians just before. If anything remains then for glorying, it must be a glorying in the Lord (*cf.* 2 Cor. 10:12-18).

5 This short statement has become proverbial, and may also give expression to an old proverb. It confirms and explains that at bottom everyone should be concerned only with his own work and not with that of others. This does not contradict verse 2. The argument now concerns a wholly different aspect of the truth and of the law of

---

[6] δοκιμάζειν: *to try,* or *to test,* often in the positive sense of: *to approve.*

[7] καύχημα: *laud,* or *praise,* or *glory,* or also that in which one glories. For Paul, usually: the possibility of glorying in self (*cf.* Rom. 4:2, 1 Cor. 9:16, and 2 Cor. 1:14; and other passages).

God.[8] Verse 2 speaks of the duty to help one another bear burdens. Verse 5 says that the guilt of another person does not excuse me. Every man is responsible for his own conduct to God. Hence, one should conduct himself as verse 4 recommends. *Burden* does not refer so much this time to the oppressive weight (as in verse 2), as to the normal duty which falls upon every man. The words *shall bear* connote the certainty of this statement, as well as the coming judgment, where it will be made manifest.

---

[8] The effort has been made in all kinds of ways to demonstrate the difference linguistically between the τὰ βάρη of verse 2 and the φορτίον of verse 5. This apparently cannot be satisfactorily done, however, and it is not necessary to eliminate contradiction.

SOWING IN THE SPIRIT

6:6-10

6 But let him that is taught in the word communicate unto him that teacheth in all good things.

7 Be not deceived; God is not mocked: for whatsoever a man soweth, that shall he also reap.

8 For he that soweth unto his own flesh shall of the flesh reap corruption; but he that soweth unto the Spirit shall of the Spirit reap eternal life.

9 And let us not be weary in well-doing: for in due season we shall reap, if we faint not.

10 So then, as we have opportunity, let us work that which is good toward all men, and especially toward them that are of the household of faith.

6 It is difficult to find the right connection between verse 6 and what precedes and what follows. In the translation given above, which we think the most accurate,[1] the pupil is encouraged to let his teacher share *in all good things.* Presumably the apostle is thinking especially of material things. As we see it one can only lay down a forced *direct* connection between this and what went be-

---

[1] Others want to translate the κοινωνείτω intransitively: to exercise fellowship. The meaning would then be: the pupil must exercise fellowship with his teacher in all good things. According to this view, these *good things* must then be given a religio-ethical content. This view would be acceptable if it could be made clear why the idea of fellowship or community issuing from the preceding argument should suddenly be applied now to the pupil-teacher relationship, indeed, be made to converge upon it as finale and climax. Moreover, the expression itself is a little too arresting for that, as is also the thought that the pupil himself should take the initiative in this, as is obviously the assumption. The thought of "taking someone as an example" simply is not in the text. Hence we choose for the interpretation described above.

fore. On the other hand, it is also difficult to suppose that the following verses, which warn of the coming judgment, are intended merely to enhance the pupil's willingness to give his teacher material support. Such would seem to be a too limited application of the following verses, especially since the opposition between Spirit and flesh comes to the fore again in verse 8, and probably has some bearing on this verse also. As it seems to us, therefore, verse 6 is a kind of independent admonition — the sort that is not at all surprising at the close of a letter. What follows thereupon gives the conclusion of all that has gone before. This conclusion is not quite lost sight of in verse 6, but is in the main something other than an introduction to it.

One can ask, finally, why Paul so emphatically raises this matter of verse 6. The concrete occasion for this admonition is not known to us, if indeed there was one. We can consider whether the foregoing material of the letter, in which the apostle pointed to the exercise of Christian fellowship as inescapable duty, is not occasion enough for touching on the neglect of duty towards the minister or teacher. Such would explain the transition. But we cannot speak with certainty of this. There is mention made in this verse of pupils and teachers. The former must share their goods with the latter.[2] This circumstance points to the fixed status of the ministers in the church.[3] The circumstance is the more remarkable because the letter to the Galatians has an early date (cf. also 1 Thess. 5:12). We do not know precisely, of course, whether this is a reference to the office of minister in the sense of an ordained service (cf. Acts 14:23), or to a voluntary function on the part of those who had received special gifts. In any event, the situation approximates the office. The term translated the word is to be specifically understood as

---

[2] For this meaning of κοινωνεῖν, see also Rom. 15:26, 2 Cor. 9:13, and Heb. 13:16.

[3] Presumably the διδάσκαλοι of 1 Cor. 12:28 and Eph. 4:11 are intended.

meaning the more detailed instruction which the churches needed after the first preaching of the gospel. See for the interpretation of *all good things* given above, also Rom. 15:27 and 1 Cor. 9:4-14.

7 The apostle now approaches the conclusion of his previously given admonitions, in which he presents with firm emphasis the gravity of the Galatians' life-choice and life-attitude. This he does in verses 7 to 9. In verse 10 he summarizes. *Be not deceived* puts his readers on the alert: they had better know what is at stake. God requires an account and He *is not mocked*: He does not permit man to make light of or to toy with the preaching of grace that comes to him and with the obligations that accompany it. The figure of sowing and reaping, too, which follows now we shall have to interpret, presumably, as in general the way in which man must live, rather than as a reference specifically to responsibility over against the minister of the word. The opposition between flesh and Spirit reminds too sharply of the whole preceding argument of the letter to permit of so limited an application. *Whatsoever a man soweth*: that is putting the thing as generally as possible; it holds for everybody, and for everything he does. The whole of earthly life is regarded as the sowing time. The harvesting — God's verdict in the judgment — will correspond to the sowing. There is natural, intimate relationship between them. This relationship is not disturbed by grace. Precisely the way in which man hears the gospel and the way in which in his practical life he deals with it is determinative of his eternal fortune.

8 The general principle of verse 7 is in this verse developed in two directions. The figure is deflected a little. The point now is not the seed that is sown but the field in which it is sown. What man is to harvest depends upon the nature of the soil in which he sows. The flesh is designated (see the Exposition of 5:16 ff.) as the field from which corruption is harvested. That which is natural and native

to man (his *own* flesh) is different from the Spirit. And he who lives for the flesh, shall reap of it. It has its own kind of fruit, namely, corruption. Corruption is not the cessation of human existence, but is the positive existence of grief and woe, temporal and eternal. That nothing less is meant is apparent also from the second clause. Whoever sows in the Spirit, devotes his life to Him and lets himself be governed by Him; he shall reap eternal life from the Spirit. For the Spirit is the grand life-giver and preserver operating through an inner law of life laid down by God. *Eternal life* speaks of the whole of life, both of body and soul, the glorified life of the resurrection on the new earth.

9 The occasion for the summons in verse 9 not to become weary[4] in doing good may be the continued delay of "the great harvest." This delay may be the cause for a lapse in the consciousness of the importance of well-doing — a cause also for the laxity and fatigue hinted here. *Well-doing*[5] is an epitome of all that is involved in walking by the Spirit, as it has been detailed in the preceding passages. Not only must the Galatians persevere in seeking to do well: they must also do it. The second clause provides the motivation: the harvest coming, however distant and tardy it may seem. However, the readers should bear in mind that this harvest will come only *in due season*: at the suitable time,[6] that is, when from God's point of view the time is ripe for it. Human judgment is deceptive about such a thing. We may sometimes think that the delay is too long. But the right time does not come until the

---

[4] For the use of ἐγκακεῖν in this context, see also Luke 18:1.

[5] καλός really means: the beautiful. It was eagerly used by the Greeks for the ethical, which is good in itself and as such evokes wonder. Here it is used in the biblical sense (*cf.* Mt. 5:16 and 26:10), measured by the divine norm, and in the sense that it can be acknowledged as good only in its manifestation. ποιεῖν stresses the result.

[6] καιρός itself designates the stipulated moment of time, in contrast with χρόνος which suggests an indeterminate period.

moment stipulated by God has arrived. And that will be harvest-time, that is, if we do not *faint*, or grow lax, in the struggle against the flesh and for the walk by the Spirit. Paul, even as Jesus (Mt. 5:12, 6:1 ff.), speaks very openly about reward and punishment, even though at this point he does not do it *ipsissimis verbis*. Of merit there is no talk at all: the statement is set in the context of the whole argument of the letter. The life of well-doing is a receiving from grace of that which God wills to give. But this acceptance stands in inseparable relationship with human responsibility.

10 The conclusion of verse 10 is that as long as[7] the time appointed for it is still at hand, the Galatians must take advantage of the opportunity zealously to work that which is good.[8] This duty should be carried out towards everyone. But there is a kind of gradation in the call to do this also. The companions of the faith, those who share the gospel, are the first to get attention. They are the nearest neighbors. But exclusivism must be avoided as conflicting with the command of God. *The household of faith*: the believers, in other words, constitute one large household, one family.

---

[7] The problem is whether we should translate the word to mean *so long as* (or while) or as *because*. The decision depends in part on what reading one chooses: ἔχωμεν or ἔχομεν. Paul generally uses no ὡς with the subjunctive unless ἄν is present. The judgment of *Bl.-Debr.* Par. 445, (2), is that we must take the ὡς here as meaning ἕως, that is, *while*. The significance of the predication is certainly first of all temporal. What is at stake is not a single occasion, however, but the whole life-span of a person. The causal significance of *as* is thereby intimated.

[8] This time the form is ἀγαθόν instead of the καλόν in verse 9: the good in a comprehensive sense, specifically expressed in a favorable bearing towards others (*cf.* 5:22).

FINAL ADMONITION. BENEDICTION

6:11-18

11 See with how large letters I write unto you with mine own hand.

12 As many as desire to make a fair show in the flesh, they compel you to be circumcised; only that they may not be persecuted for the cross of Christ.

13 For not even they who receive circumcision do themselves keep the law; but they desire to have you circumcised, that they may glory in your flesh.

14 But far be it from me to glory, save in the cross of our Lord Jesus Christ, through which the world has been crucified unto me, and I unto the world.

15 For neither is circumcision anything, nor uncircumcision, but a new creature.

16 And as many as shall walk by this rule, peace *be* upon them, and mercy, and upon the Israel of God.

17 Henceforth let no man trouble me; for I bear branded on my body the marks of Jesus.

18 The grace of our Lord Jesus Christ be with your spirit, brethren. Amen.

11 The apostle has arrived at the concluding portion of his letter. The first thing he does is to call attention to the large letters[1] with which he is writing. Presumably we are to limit these to this conclusion rather than to think

---

[1] The translation is not quite sure. γράμματα can also mean *letter* (epistle). It is rather generally accepted, however, that *letters* is the right version. For one thing the epistle is not a very long one. For another thing, we would then expect the accusative. And, finally, Paul always uses the word ἐπιστολή for letter.

of them in connection with the whole letter.[2] Paul made use of the services of a scribe. The signature would be in his own hand (*cf.* 1 Cor. 16:21 ff., Col. 4:18, and 2 Thess. 3:17). The reference to the large letters is nothing more than a sign-post announcing that at this point the conclusion of the letter, done in his own hand, begins. This is not only to earmark the whole letter as genuine, but it is also to press these summarizing and conclusive words in upon the consciences of his readers as intensely as possible.

Various opinions have been expressed about the large characters of Paul's penmanship. Some regard them as evidence of his inexperience in writing. Others think they can establish the fact that in those days large letters amounted to the same thing as underscoring or italicizing. The idea, on that basis is, that Paul deliberately made the letters stand out boldly. It is possible also, however, that Paul's writing was distinguished by a certain robustness and vigor, or that he is deliberately writing large characters at this point to distinguish his own hand from that of his scribe. We shall have to be careful in drawing final conclusions in this matter.

12 The verse leads to a final sharp attack upon the Judaizers. The apostle disparages not only their action, but also their motives. They want to cut a good figure,[3] want to be popular with people. And they want this *in the flesh,* that is, externally. The idea is that those who

---

[2] In other words we are to look upon the ἔγραψα not as a real but as an epistolary preterit. Others think that Paul is speaking of the letters or characters of the whole letter. In that event, we should be dealing with a real preterit, and Paul would have to be assumed as writing the whole letter. The reference to the large characters would then be intended to call the attention of the Galatians to the fact that Paul, whose hands, because of his travelling and manual labor, were not suited to penmanship, was going to considerable pains in writing this message. But it may well be questioned whether the evidence here warrants all these inferences.

[3] εὐπροσωπέω: used only at this point in the New Testament.

compel[4] circumcision are making a bid for the favor of the people, particularly of the Jews of the dispersion. Their whole purpose in doing so, however, is to escape persecution. Paul brings the cross of Christ into this context in a particular way. This cross is the cause of the persecution which the Judaizers fear. For the preaching of the cross speaks of the sufficiency of Christ's work, and of the superfluousness of circumcision. *To be persecuted* is a general term comprehending the enmity, opposition, and threats to life brought to bear by influential Jews against the radical preaching of Christ (*cf.* Acts 13:45, 50; 14:2, 5, and 19, and other passages). Those who modified the preaching of Jesus by some attention to the Jewish institutions, and propagated such a modified preaching, were apparently not persecuted by such Jews. For thus the exclusive significance of Judaism remained primary.

13 Those *who receive circumcision*[5] refers, as is evident from the second clause, to the heretical teachers themselves. That these had to be referred to in so disparaging a sense as in verse 12 becomes clear (*for*) from this, too, that they themselves do not take the law, about which they raise such a fanfare, very seriously. Presumably Paul is not alluding so much to the general inability of man to keep the law as to the hypocrisy and practical expediencies to which precisely these foremost proponents of the law sometimes took recourse (*cf.* Mt. 23 and Lk. 11:46). The real motive of these Judaistic zealots is selfish pride. They want to boast of the fact that they have brought Gentiles by descent to the point of circumcision. They want this

---

[4] ἀναγκάζουσιν: *de conatu.*

[5] The reading περιτετμημένοι, as it is found in P[46] and B probably is owing to scribal correction. The reference is to the heretical teachers themselves (see the Exposition). The perfect tense would seem to be more appropriate than the present tense. Hence the variant. The present, although it offers difficulty, must be taken in a very general sense: "the circumcision-people," "those who favor circumcision."

simply to flatter their own chauvinistic legalism. They want to glory in the Galatian Gentiles before others. That these circumcised Gentiles would also want to be Christians does not matter. By their circumcision they would have knuckled under to Judaism. *That they might glory in your flesh*: their egoistic effort is accomplished at the cost of others. Paul states this as concretely as possible,[6] so as to give the Galatians the true and fundamentally intolerable earmark of the heretical teachers.

14 Very emphatically the apostle sets his own effort in contrast to theirs. So he demonstrates not only that he absolutely despises the motives and purposes of his opponents,[7] but also that he glories in something too. But this thing in which he glories constitutes a threat to those who seek themselves. The cross of Christ is his glory. It is a paradoxical thing to glory in, for it is almost an image of weakness and misery (*cf.* 1 Cor. 1:18 ff.). Paul, however, presents this glory of the cross by naming it with the fulness and richness of Christ's names, as he and his readers may know and confess them. Hence, too, the fitness of the next clause: *through which the world hath been crucified unto me.* The *world* as used here is an epitome of everything outside of Christ in which man seeks his glory and puts his trust. The contrast is in the first place presumably directed against the Judaizers. Their glorying, Paul says in effect, is worldly, godless, vain, however religious it may seem to be. But beyond that the *world* points to everything in the world in its length and breadth and variation, on which man in his vanity trusts, and in which he glories. Because of the cross this whole world

---

[6] σαρκί points to circumcision: the circumcised organ.

[7] The construction, "Far be it from me," is used in the Old Testament also in this form (*cf.* Josh. 22:29, 24:16: LXX). It stands about half-way between a prayer and a curse.

has been crucified for Paul. He has written it off as a basis for glorying and trust. Christ teaches him to turn his back upon all other things, however, desirable and mighty they may be. The word *to crucify* points to the absoluteness of the contrast. The glory of the world is absolutely, radically objectionable; it is dead, obliterated (*cf.* Phil. 3:7, 8). This fact has a subjective as well as an objective aspect: *and I unto the world*. In him, too, that crucifying takes the place of everything that went out to the world as a basis for vindication and trust. Because he has learned to put all his hope and confidence in Christ, the world has nothing with which to charm him and bind him to itself. In these words the deepest chords of the Pauline *kerygma* are sounded. Paul speaks here of the cross as the one and sufficient ground on which to build; he also speaks of his own life as of something entirely governed by the cross. Thus, the element of judgment is present also in *hath been crucified*. Both the world and the human confidence in it have become manifest not only in their inadequacy but also in their damnableness. The person who lives for the world will together with it be destroyed. By the cross the believer is saved from this destruction. This crucifying of the world and of the self in mutual interdependence means life and redemption for him who has learned to direct his life solely upon the cross of Christ.

15 This whole matter is now motivated in greater detail, again by reference to the question of circumcision. The Judaizers gloried in that. And to this concrete point Paul returns, after his consideration of the general concept of *the world*. This verse reminds us very much of 5:6 (see Exposition of it), and also of 1 Cor. 7:19. Neither circumcision nor uncircumcision is of any value as a basis for vindication and salvation: what matters is being *a* *new creature.* The words point to the new life[5] in the Holy Spirit. Such a life consists of a faithful appropriation of the new relationship to God. But the expression speaks also of the subjective renewal of life, a renewal which has the earmarks of re-creation, of regeneration. It forms the secret source and principle of a new life-form. *New* includes everything that has been given in and through Christ — the new reality of the kingdom of God. Through Christ this new thing is not merely future-eschatological (Rev. 21:1-5, 3:12 and Mark 14:25) but is already present, is already *in* man. This new creation is first of all a gift, but it brings its task with it. This whole matter, then, is the one thing that counts. In this new salvation, brought by Christ, lies the source of the glorying and of the zeal that is necessary. And over against this thing, the old thing, circumcision is no longer useful. What counts is circumcision of the heart (Rom. 2:29), the gift of the Spirit, the earmark and the guarantee of the new covenant (*cf.* Heb. 8:8 ff.).

16 As is evident from the benediction at the end of this verse, the apostle now arrives at the end of his argument. *This rule* comprehends everything he has said. It points to the new norm and measure. The cross of Christ forms its point of departure, and the new creature forms its realization. Everything must be measured by its standard. It is the norm for what matters, for what is valid and what is not, for what is to be accepted and what is to be rejected. *To walk by*[9] this rule means that in thought and action alike the Galatians are to be guided by their disposition towards that rule. For all to whom this proves to be applicable, the benediction is also applicable.

---

[8] κτίσις can refer either to the divine act or to its product. Here it is very probably being used in the latter sense (*cf.* 5:6, 1 Cor. 7:19, 2 Cor. 5:17). Still it is not to be taken in the general sense of *man,* but, as is clear also from the added καινή in the full significance of a creature of God (*cf.* Eph. 2:10, 15, 4:24, Col. 3:10, and James 1:18).

[9] See the Exposition of 5:25.

This benediction reminds greatly of the well-known Jewish *Shemoneh Esre* (the Eighteen-petition prayer): "Grant peace, salvation, and blessing, grant favor, grace, and mercy to us and to all Israel, thy people." The benediction speaks of *peace*, presumably to be understood here in the general and comprehensive sense of the eschatological salvation (see Exposition of 5:22). It speaks of *mercy*, that is, the grace which God has promised His people in His covenant[10] and which Israel therefore expects from God. In other words, the benediction speaks of the great gift of salvation promised by God and granted in principle by Christ. Such a perspective is very appropriate at the end of a letter which again and again spoke of the receiving of the inheritance promised to the seed of Abraham (3:18, 29; 5:21). Somewhat surprising is the addition: *and upon the Israel of God.* In view of what has gone before (*cf.* 3:29, 4:28, 29) we can hardly doubt that this *Israel of God* does not refer to the empirical, national Israel as an equally authorized partner *alongside of* the believers in Christ ("they who walk by this rule"). As elsewhere (*cf.* Rom. 9:7), so here, Israel designates the new Israel. In this benediction, then, the apostle has the readers of his letter, in so far as they walk by the new rule, in mind, but from them its scope goes out to include in the widest sense all believers whatsoever, the new people of God. All the same, the expression retains a surprising element, because Paul does not generally speak of Israel in this special sense, without further explanation. The occasion for doing so now may have been the traditional Jewish prayer, in which there is reference to *us* first, and then to *all Israel, thy people.* The apostle is, in other words, making use of a relationship lying ready in his mind. It is a relationship, however, which in his preaching was given a new content because of the new development in the history of salvation.

---

[10] ἔλεος is the equivalent of the Old Testament חֶסֶד

17 Finally Paul asks that *henceforth*[11] he may be spared the trouble caused him, not so much by the Judaistic zealots (for he can hardly lodge an appeal with them), but by the churches who because of the zealots permitted themselves to be deflected from the truth in Christ. In this connection, Paul appeals to *the marks*[12] *of Jesus* which he bears. Presumably these are the marks of suffering and affliction which had accrued to him in the service of the gospel. They are called marks *of Jesus,* not because Paul received the same wounds in his body which Jesus received, but because in these tokens his fellowship in suffering with Jesus becomes manifest (*cf.* 2 Cor. 4:10, Phil. 3:10, Rom. 8:17, 2 Cor. 1:5, and Col. 1:24). This demonstrates also that what the believers must suffer at the hands of the world's enmity is the same thing that Jesus had to undergo — not the same in its fruit, but in its nature. Incidentally, this suffering is more than an affliction for the sake of or in consequence of following Jesus. A certain transfer of suffering from Jesus to the believers takes place by virtue of the fellowship, the corporative and federal oneness existing between them. In this passage, the marks are especially the marks of Jesus, too, because they point to what happened to Jesus in his earthly life. The marks which Paul bears must serve to warn those who cause Paul so much trouble and grief. They are then assailing someone who has put his life in the service of the Lord, and who bears the brands of that

---

[11] τοῦ λοιποῦ (*sc.* χρόνου) is an adverb of time: *in the future* (in distinction from τὸ λοιπόν: "for the rest").

[12] τὰ στίγματα: The word *stigmatization* is derived from this word in the sense of exhibiting the wounds of Christ (Francis of Assisi, for example, and Therese Neumann). Some have tried to relate the phenomenon of stigmata with Gal. 6:17. But this has been done without basis, as Roman Catholic exegetes and dogmatic scholars also acknowledge. See also Oepke, *op. cit.,* p. 124.

service.[13] And there certainly lies in this statement also the implication that in doing so they are opposing Jesus Himself, and inviting the punishment of God upon them.

18 The letter ends with a closing blessing. There are no personal greetings or other personal particulars, as in so many other letters. One can ask whether this tersely economical conclusion reflects the tensions of the whole situation, even as the economical introduction does so. But one can hardly speak with certainty about it. We can say simply that this short and unprepared for conclusion leaves the readers under the full force of the gripping admonition of the letter. This, of course, helps to press it home upon their consciences. For the rest, this conclusion is very cordial, and winsome in its manner. It has a hearty, ingratiating quality; there is nothing of irritation in it. The last word before the stately *Amen* is the nominative *brethren.* Despite all and in and through everything Paul clings to communion with them in Christ. To that, too, he makes his last appeal. Thereupon he wishes them *the grace of our Lord Jesus Christ.* The grace represents the summary and the presupposition of all that Christ gives. The notion of the unearned, the undeserved, is contained in it. And also the fulness of this good, this salvation, now and in eternity. Once more he mentions all the names of the Lord. They emphasize His glory, His saving significance, and His divine commission, respectively. This

---

[13]Some think that Paul is alluding here to a cultic use of religious tattooing. By this means people dedicated themselves to the deity. The mark was therefore a kind of brand-mark, or mark of property, and also a mark of protection. In time the mark took on the significance of an amulet. The technical term for such tattooing was στίγμα. Although it is difficult for us to make out what readers of that time saw in such a word, it seems to us unwarranted to regard Paul's marks as "cult-marks of the Exalted One," designating Paul the "property" of Christ. The subject at this point is the fellowship in suffering with Christ, not cultic property rights, even though the language employed could owe something to certain pagan practices.

grace, Paul says, *be with your spirit.* May it move the Galatians in the whole of their inner being, so that they are wholly informed by it, put all their trust in it, and conduct themselves according to it. The stately *Amen* is not simply a confirmation coming from Paul's side, but involves the readers in its import also, even as it does in a prayer or doxology at worship, when the minister speaks it also in the name of the auditors.

INDEX

INDEX OF CHIEF SUBJECTS

INDEX OF SCRIPTURE REFERENCES

OLD TESTAMENT

DE

A